HELEN STEINER RICE—
The
Healing Touch

Also by Ronald Pollitt and Virginia Wiltse

Helen Steiner Rice: Ambassador of Sunshine
The Rock and the River: Helen Steiner Rice—Her Life and Poetry
  (audio)

HELEN STEINER RICE—

The
Healing Touch

Poems, Letters, and Life Stories

**Ronald Pollitt
and Virginia Wiltse**

Fleming H. Revell
A Division of Baker Book House
Grand Rapids, Michigan 49516

Published by Fleming H. Revell
a division of Baker Book House Company
P.O. Box 6287, Grand Rapids, MI 49516-6287

Printed in the United States of America

Library of Congress Cataloging-in-Publication Data

Pollitt, Ronald.
    Helen Steiner Rice—the healing touch : poems, letters, and life stories / Ronald Pollitt and Virginia Wiltse.
      p.   cm.
    ISBN 0-8007-1750-3 (cloth)
    1. Rice, Helen Steiner—Appreciation. 2. Women poets, American—20th century—Correspondence. 3. Christian poetry, American—History and criticism. 4. Christian poetry, American. 5. Adjustment (Psychology).
    6. Spiritual life. I. Rice, Helen Steiner. II. Wiltse, Virginia, 1949– . III. Title.
PS3568.I28Z84   1998
811'.54—dc21   97-51205

Sincere appreciation to Eileen Annest for the use of her portrait of Helen Steiner Rice on page 14.

For current information about all releases from Baker Book House, visit our web site:

http://www.bakerbooks.com

Contents

List of Poems   7

Foreword   9

Acknowledgments   11

Twelve Healing Attitudes of Helen Steiner Rice   13

1. The Healing Touch   15
2. Healing the Pain of Loss   35
3. Healing the Pain of Adversity   61
4. Healing the Pain of Loneliness   87
5. Healing the Pain of Depression   117
6. Healing the Pain of Disability   147
7. Healing the Pain of Infirmity   173
8. Your Healing Touch   201

Afterword   215

List of Poems

Before You Can Dry Another's Tears—You Too Must Weep!   17
A Child's Faith   24
The Better You Know God, the Better You Feel   26
There Is a Reason for Everything   39
Nothing on Earth Is Forever Yours—
    Only the Love of the Lord Endures!   47
All Nature Tells Us Nothing Really Ever Dies   52
When I Must Leave You   55
Let Not Your Heart Be Troubled   64
Daily Prayers Dissolve Your Cares   75
Storms Bring Out the Eagles but the Little Birds Take Cover   78
Each Day Brings a Chance to Do Better   83
Everybody Needs Someone   88
This Too Will Pass Away   92
My Daily Prayer   99
Brighten the Corner Where You Are   106
God Is Never Beyond Our Reach   114
The End of the Road Is but a Bend in the Road   121
Seasons of the Soul   125
Under New Management   127
There's Always a Springtime   134

Never Be Discouraged   136
When Trouble Comes and Things Go Wrong!   138
Burdens Are Things God Turns into Wings   141
A Sure Way to a Happy Day   152
The Way to God   163
On the Wings of Prayer   165
Blessings in Disguise Are Difficult to Recognize   168
Believe   176
Give Me the Contentment of Acceptance   184
Growing Older Is Part of God's Plan   189
Prayers Can't Be Answered Unless They Are Prayed   193
Dark Shadows Fall in the Lives of Us All   195
Golden Years of Life   197
With His Love   202
The Master Builder   205
A Prayer for Humility   205
The Soul of Man   212
There Are Blessings in Everything   219

Foreword

od sends messengers as we need them, individuals whose great devotion to their calling is matched to their placement in time and space. Such people are able to be of benefit to many in the service of God's creation. I regard Helen Steiner Rice as such a messenger who is especially appropriate for us at the end of the twentieth century.

In her life, which spanned most of the century, Helen Steiner Rice witnessed with dismay the growing dominance of profit and power-driven materialistic culture in this country and elsewhere, and was among the many who personally suffered from its imbalances. She also suffered through the experience of living in her body, which (in kinship with many of our era) underwent painful degeneration over time. Her courageous response to the trials of her life became the basis of her poetry, which came from her wounded healer's heart.

Helen found through honoring her suffering and facing it head on, open-heartedly, that she was able to (day by day) come into a deeper realization of the essential nature of human life. She saw our earthly existence as a continuum of opportunities to come into our true sense of self, through encountering and transcending those experiences that could engross us in pain, isolation, and despair. She repeated this work constantly through seeking God's love and peace within herself and in other people, seeing that our compassionate care of each other is a royal road to the divine.

Mrs. Rice's life and writings deeply affected many people directly, as *The Healing Touch* eloquently portrays. The poetry and life of Helen Steiner Rice, so steeped in her Christianity, so Christ-like, transcends sectarian limitations. She is a psalmist who brings fluency to our religious cacophony and she does it in lovely, simple, broadly accessible language. Her poems take us deeply within ourselves to rekindle the light of our souls, the manifestation of God in our lives, as experienced individually and communally. She reminds us that we are loved and that our experience of our spirituality in our bodies is the fundamental task of our earthly existence, to hallow God's name on earth as it is in heaven. And she reminds us through the poetry of her life how to accomplish this task, day by day.

I wish to thank the authors for their work of bringing the universal healing message of Helen Steiner Rice to a broader sharing. It is my hope that readers of this and other books by and about Mrs. Rice will, as I have, find sweet reward for their investment.

Henry F. Kennel, M.D.
Medical Director
Franciscan Wholistic Health Center
Cincinnati, Ohio

Acknowledgments

We gratefully acknowledge the patience and assistance of Pamela Pollitt, C.P.A., and David Wiltse, M.D., during the preparation of this book. We also appreciate the enthusiasm for the project extended by the Helen Steiner Rice Foundation. In particular we thank Virginia J. Ruehlmann and Dorothy Lingg at the Foundation offices for making it possible for us to contact many of the people whose stories became a vital part of this book.

Finally, we thank those who shared with us by letter, by telephone, and in person stories about the way Helen Steiner Rice has touched their lives. We have been inspired by all of them. Helen would undoubtedly agree with us that they are the true heroes and heroines of this book.

Twelve
Healing Attitudes
of Helen Steiner Rice

1. God loves you. You are never outside God's care.

2. God hears your every prayer. You are never alone if you can talk to God.

3. God works through you. Loving yourself and others is God at work.

4. God's plan is unfolding even when you do not understand it. Surrender your will to God.

5. God's grace is always found in the present moment. Stay focused on the present.

6. God has not asked only you to cope with problems. They are part of every person's life. Refuse to indulge in self-pity.

7. Rid yourself of negative thinking. You cannot enjoy life when you are filled with complaints.

8. Be grateful for your many blessings.

9. Be kind. Acts of kindness transform the world.

10. Support one another. All of us are a valued part of God's creation.

11. Be cheerful. Happiness is a choice you make every day.

12. Learn from adversity. Your troubles are great teachers.

One

The Healing Touch

Let me not live a life that's free
From the things that draw me close to Thee,
For how can I ever hope to heal
The wounds of others I do not feel?

Helen Steiner Rice spent the better part of her life healing the wounds of others. She healed, as the stories in this book will reveal, not with science, medication, or technology. Rather, she healed with words and wisdom, with faith and love. In her prayers she did not ask for a pain-free life, but for one that would draw her closer to God and others. Helen's prayers were answered, and from the suffering of her own life she learned to touch the soul pain of those around her so their healing could begin. She healed because she felt the wounds and pain of others as her own. The word *compassion* comes from Latin words meaning to suffer together. By being a companion to others in their suffering, Helen showed true compassion.

In his book *The Wounded Healer* Henri Nouwen suggests that anyone who would be a "soul healer" in the modern world should follow the example of Jesus Christ. That individual must not only heal his or her own wounds, but must also turn them into a source of healing for others. This certainly describes the lifework of Helen Steiner Rice. She lost her loved ones and her dreams; she suffered financial reverses and unjust accusations; she endured loneliness, depression, disability, and infirmity. Her poetry sprang from her personal heartaches and her attempts not only to heal them, but also to learn from them. Her search for meaning from the life experiences that wounded her led Helen Steiner Rice into the mystery of God's love. She chose to make her pain a teacher and not a conqueror. As a result she became a wounded healer, a woman who, because she honestly attended to her own wounds, was able to transform her sorrow into a source of healing for others. In the end this work became her greatest joy.

The life, the letters, and the poetry of Helen Steiner Rice suggest a pattern that Helen followed again and again for healing herself and others. When she faced heartache, she always asked, What can I learn? When she encountered difficulties and disappointments, she looked for opportunities to grow in wisdom. She lived her faith in God literally: When she could not logically understand the events of her life, she let go of the need to understand and placed the results in God's hands. Finally, she chose the attitude of the healer: She transcended her own pain so that she might help others survive their suffering. At the same time, she was blessed with the God-given talent to put into words that everyone can understand her feelings about facing up to any calamity. This book is filled with stories of people who learned from Helen's example and in doing so healed themselves and others. Helen sparked a mysterious quality in all of them that made it possible for them to resolve, "I will not let this defeat me. God loves me and I can go on."

The Wounds of the Healer

The process of transmuting pain into healing did not take place overnight for Helen Steiner Rice. Unfolding throughout her life, it began and continued mostly because she committed

Before You Can Dry Another's Tears—
You Too Must Weep!

Let me not live a life that's free
From "the things" that draw me close to Thee—
For how can I ever hope to heal
The wounds of others I do not feel—
If my eyes are dry and I never weep,
How do I know when the hurt is deep—
If my heart is cold and it never bleeds,
How can I tell what my brother needs—
For when ears are deaf to the beggar's plea
And we close our eyes and refuse to see,
And we steel our hearts and harden our minds,
And we count it a weakness whenever we're kind,
We are no longer following the Father's Way
Or seeking His guidance from day to day—
For, without "crosses to carry" and "burdens to bear,"
We dance through a life that is frothy and fair,
And "chasing the rainbow" we have no desire
For "roads that are rough" and "realms that are
    higher"—
So spare me no heartache or sorrow, dear Lord,
For the heart that is hurt reaps the richest reward,
And God enters the heart that is broken with sorrow
As He opens the door to a Brighter Tomorrow,
For only through tears can we recognize
The suffering that lies in another's eyes.

herself time and again to a journey through life in faith, despite the most bewildering and stressful circumstances. "Thy will, not mine, be done" became a lifelong theme of her prayers and poems. She developed the capacity simply to accept what she could not comprehend.

This attitude of acceptance did not represent resignation or indicate defeat. On the contrary, it signaled her growth in true wisdom. Helen always had a positive outlook but as she learned how to accept life's troubles as part of a divine process, she also developed the ability to calm confusion and turmoil in others who struggled with their own problems. "Before you can dry another's tears, you too must weep," Helen wrote. Nothing could be more true. Yet there was more than weeping that led her to resolve her own inner conflicts in a way that enabled her to ease the pain of others. Determination and personal discipline played a key part. "I have no creed but Christ," she often said. As a faithful reader of the Bible, she knew that Christ himself did battle with the devil before he drove the demons out of others.

It seems as though each phase of Helen's life presented her with new battles to fight, and from the wounds of those battles she learned certain crucial lessons about healing the human spirit. This book is organized around six of the wounds that became sources of strength as Helen Steiner Rice touched the lives of others.

Loss

Helen's compassion for the bereaved, her sensitivity, and her kindness drew the attention and admiration of coworkers and friends alike. She rarely failed to write them poems of understanding and consolation in times of distress. She knew the pain of loss all too well. Helen's father died suddenly when she was eighteen years old and just out of high school. A healthy, vibrant man who worked on the railroad, her father fell ill during the 1918 influenza epidemic and died a few days later. She was shattered by the loss of a parent she had adored and found comfort in the words of a friend who encouraged her to keep his memory alive by exemplifying the principles of service and selflessness he had taught her.

The loss of her father also robbed Helen of cherished dreams and goals. It destroyed her plans for college and law school. After her father died, Helen became the sole support of her mother and sister, working first as a lampshade designer, then in public relations. The death of her father taught Helen that loss was part of the cycle of life. If one could adjust to it, accept it, and learn from it, then something new would grow and the eternal pattern of death, life, and renewal would complete itself.

Adversity

When Helen married at the age of twenty-nine, she had every reason to expect that a life of ease and leisure awaited her. Franklin Rice, a wealthy Dayton, Ohio, banker, promised her every material thing she could desire. Not long after their wedding, however, he lost his entire fortune in the Great Depression. Left in poverty, they even had to borrow money for groceries. To make matters worse, while Helen searched desperately for work, her brother-in-law heartlessly accused her of sabotaging Franklin's future. Despite her part-time jobs, the couple sank ever deeper in debt.

Helen finally took a job in Cincinnati with the Gibson Art Company, but Franklin, unable to find employment himself, despaired and finally committed suicide. Helen found herself in the awful position of having to contend with her husband's death as well as with a mountain of unpaid bills. Neither of these adversities was due to any shortcoming of her own. The temptation was great, however, to blame herself for failing to understand Franklin's state of mind and take steps to avert the disaster. In the end, rather than cast blame, complain, or succumb to self-pity, Helen chose to accept in faith the circumstances that had forced her to change her expectations of life. She adjusted, she learned, and she got on with what she realized was the life God had given her. Her own adverse circumstances made Helen more sensitive to the pain of others. To them she often wrote about concentrating on what is rather than what might have been or what never will be.

Loneliness

Helen Steiner Rice lived alone in a hotel for nearly fifty years. She was widowed at the age of thirty-two and had no children. Her only sister lived over two hundred miles away in another city. Helen often felt lonely and she openly acknowledged periods of what she called the "lost-loneliness" that sooner or later comes to all people. In letters to her friends, however, she distinguished between being solitary and being lonely. Even though she lived by herself, Helen remained connected to others through social interaction, the telephone, and correspondence. Helen also knew that if she prayed, she certainly was not alone. God was present, listening to her, loving her.

Helen faced another kind of loneliness as well, the loneliness of alienation. She described it quite clearly when in the early 1950s she visited Europe during a vacation. The other Americans in her group always seemed to be jovial and never tired of celebrating. In the midst of the crowd Helen felt utterly estranged, mostly because all she could see was the devastation that had been wrought by World War II. Consequently when teenagers wrote to her saying they felt they did not fit in, Helen understood. So many things in the world made no sense to her, but blaming others for her feelings of alienation was not in her character. Helen faced alienation by asking herself what she needed to change in her own perceptions so she could feel in harmony with life once again. In this way she cultivated her connections to God and to others.

Depression

Even though those around her perceived Helen Steiner Rice as cheerful and optimistic, she never tried to gloss over the fact that periods of sadness are a normal part of the human condition, that everyone faces times of darkness and disappointment. For example, a sense of powerlessness to stop what seemed to her pointless and insensitive changes that caused suffering—both in the world at large and in her own circle—ushered in a period of depression for Helen in the years immediately after World War II. She lamented that business, in its headlong rush for profits, no longer treated workers with dignity and concern. She feared that kindness was being replaced by efficiently soulless technology and she was sadly frustrated in her efforts to prevent close friends from losing their jobs. At the same time she struggled with the physical and emotional changes that accompanied menopause. Helen also recognized periods of spiritual depression, times when she felt God made her increasingly aware of her own weakness so that she might trust more completely in the divine plan.

She countered depression with creativity, gratefulness, and compassion. In time the feelings of powerlessness in the 1940s and 1950s led her to begin writing to friends her first rhymed Christmas messages in personal greeting cards that encouraged these friends to heal the pain in the world through simple acts of love. Everyone might not have the economic power of the mighty corporation, she reasoned, but everyone did have the power to transmit love through ordinary acts of kindness. Moreover, Helen faced all forms of sadness by honestly addressing what was going on inside her and asking, Am I simply indulging in self-pity? If the answer was yes, then she dealt with the problem directly by using grateful, positive thoughts to combat the self-defeating, negative ones.

Disability

Helen suffered from a degenerative disease that affected the vertebrae in her back. For years she lived and worked in chronic pain. She began many days by soaking in a tub filled with the hottest water she could endure, just to make her body supple enough for her to dress and go in to her office. Because of that affliction, Helen could readily empathize with those who wrote to her because they sought relief from physical suffering. Two things she did not do, however, were complain and feel sorry for herself. She described her physical ailments as "gifts of God's love," lessons that taught her things about herself she could not have learned otherwise. She claimed, for example, that the limp she developed as a result of her back problems made her aware of how vain she had been all her life.

Helen witnessed disability not only through the experience of the one who suffers, but also through the eyes of the one who tries without success to relieve the pain of a relative or friend. She invested a great deal of her time, understanding, concern, and even financial resources in those who needed support. She encouraged caregivers to turn their frustrations over to God and urged them to recognize how many lessons they could learn from things they could not change.

Infirmity

Helen lived independently most of her life, so depending on others during her final years left her feeling vulnerable. Once able to walk to church, shops, and social occasions, near the end of her life she had to rely on others to get around at all. When her back deteriorated, Helen needed her sister's help even to get into her back brace. Rather than let herself be overcome by self-pity, Helen tried to remain as active as possible. She continued to work, write poetry, and correspond with friends until she was nearly eighty. It frustrated her terribly when age forced her to slow down, for she wanted to "spread the Great Story" of God's love, to stay in touch with the disheartened, and to write new poems! Toward the end, she acknowledged that slowing down was what God wanted her to do. She had surrendered her will to God years earlier but by this time she realized this important act needed renewing every single day.

As her body failed her, Helen faced other trials that reminded her of a growing dependence on others. The hotel where she had lived for decades was demolished to make way for renovations in the city center. Forced out of her home at the age of seventy-four, Helen decided that she simply had to trust that God would give her what she needed—in this case, a new place to live. Her faith was rewarded when a friend found her a new apartment a few blocks away. Trusting that God would always provide the right solution became Helen's response to her growing limitations. And until the right solution appeared, Helen chose to be cheerful rather than discouraged and content rather than complaining.

Throughout her life Helen Steiner Rice made the choices of a faith-filled healer. Not surprisingly, those around her loved her, for she was a loyal, compassionate friend and they benefited from her presence; and once the public at large recognized the value of her personal message, the "healing touch" of Helen Steiner Rice spread around the world.

A Reputation for Healing

Although Helen began as early as the 1930s writing verses to cheer and comfort people, it was not until 1960, when she was sixty years old, that her poems came to the attention of the general public. After her poems were read on the Lawrence Welk television show to a national audience, Helen's popularity soared almost overnight. Thousands immediately recognized the wisdom of her simple, everyday language, but what astounded Helen was the incredible demand for her poems that followed. Her office was deluged by an extraordinary variety of letters. Some praised her work, others congratulated her on expressing feelings for which they had no outlet, and just as many thanked her for the gift of a new way to deal with their problems.

From the very beginning many of her admirers found a source of healing in Helen's verses and they wrote to thank her and seek her advice. "Dear Beautiful, Wonderful Lady," one letter began; "God, through you, has worked a miracle." Another

A Child's Faith

"Jesus loves me, this I know,
For the BIBLE tells me so."
Little children ask no more,
For love is all they're looking for,
And in a small child's shining eyes
The FAITH of all the ages lies
And tiny hands and tousled heads
That kneel in prayer by little beds
Are closer to the dear Lord's heart
And of His Kingdom more a part
Than we who search, and never find
The answers to our questioning mind
For faith in things we cannot see
Requires a child's simplicity
For, lost in life's complexities
We drift upon uncharted seas
And slowly FAITH disintegrates
While wealth and power accumulates—
And the more man learns, the less he knows,
And the more involved his thinking grows
And, in his arrogance and pride,
No longer is man satisfied
To place his confidence and love
With childlike FAITH in God above—
Oh, Father, grant once more to men
A simply childlike FAITH again
And, with a small child's trusting eyes,
May all men come to realize
That FAITH alone can save man's soul
And lead him to a HIGHER GOAL.

described her as a "radiating center for God's love"; still another as simply "an angel."

Ever honest with herself, Helen was surprised by the response to her verses. She had always written, as she put it, simply out of her own "deeply thankful heart." Practical, faith-filled, and humble, Helen knew what had happened was an answer to prayer. She had prayed to God every day for decades, "Make me a channel of blessing today." God had answered! Now her poems were reminding others of God's constant presence and encouraging them to make the necessary changes in their attitudes that would enable them to reduce suffering and facilitate healing.

The more Helen wrote, the more people hungered for her work. Her message always sprang from the personal experience of pain and the healing that followed. Like all talented writers, she wrote about what she knew best, what she had discovered in the course of living—challenges enter our lives not to embitter us, but to heal us of our wrong thinking and teach us that joy transcends earthly comfort. Life is a divine lesson, and every obstacle offers us a choice. By tending her own wounds and learning from her own heartaches, Helen Steiner Rice became, as she had so often prayed, "a channel of blessing" in the lives of others.

The Power of Faith

Helen Steiner Rice's poems of the 1960s and 1970s are all founded on the premise that mind, body, and soul are inextricably connected. Now, a quarter of a century later, Helen's intuitive grasp of how everything works together has been affirmed by medical, psychological, and spiritual experts. The core messages that found life in the experiences of an inspirational writer from Cincinnati and won the hearts of millions of ordinary folks now fill professional journals and make headlines as cover stories in spiritual and secular magazines alike—"Scientists Discover What Believers Have Always Known: Prayer Heals," "Pos-

The Better You Know God, the Better You Feel

The better you know God, the better you feel,
For to learn and discover and know God is real
Can wholly, completely and miraculously change,
Reshape and remake and then rearrange
Your mixed-up, miserable and unhappy life
"Adrift on the sea of sin-sickened strife"—
But once you know Christ, this "Man of good will,"
Will calm your life and say "Peace, be still" . . .
So open your "heart's door" and let Christ come in
And He'll give you new life and free you from sin—
And there is no joy that can ever compare
With the joy of knowing you're in God's care.

itive Emotions Counter the Harmful Effects of Negative Thinking," "Kindness Linked to Health Benefits." Helen would probably be amused to learn that what seemed so obvious to her now makes news. On the other hand, she might also be relieved to know that people are finally taking spiritual well-being seriously and recognizing it as the powerful force she understood it to be.

For Helen, belief in God was indispensable to living a happy, healthy life, which she clearly expressed in the poem "The Better You Know God, the Better You Feel."

> The better you know God, the better you feel,
> For to learn and discover and know God is real
> Can wholly, completely and miraculously change,
> Reshape and remake and then rearrange
> Your mixed-up, miserable and unhappy life. . . .

Scholars such as F. C. Craigie and others reviewed medical literature over a ten-year period and found an overwhelmingly positive connection between spiritual commitment and the status of a person's health. Their work was published in 1990. By 1995 two other researchers, Dale Matthews and David Larson, enumerated 160 subsequent studies that demonstrated a positive correlation between getting well and having a religious commitment. The findings of such respected experts leave no doubt that Helen Steiner Rice's approach has merit. Developing a relationship with God can clearly have an important impact on our lives.

According to Helen, prayer can be just as powerful as faith. Her poem "Daily Prayers Dissolve Your Cares" tells us that expressing your thoughts not only restores a sense of balance, but it also renews your strength.

> . . . in the stillness of the night
> Before sleep comes I pray
> That God will just "take over"
> All the problems I couldn't solve
> And in the peacefulness of sleep

My cares will all dissolve,
So when I open up my eyes
To greet another day
I'll find myself renewed in strength
And there'll open up a way
To meet what seemed impossible
For me to solve alone
And once again I'll be assured
I am never "on my own."

The recent book *Healing Words* by Dr. Larry Dossey describes the real benefits of prayer both to the one who prays and to the one for whom prayer is offered. One of those benefits is the affirmation that simply by praying we acknowledge that we are not alone. Dr. Dossey's conclusions are supported by the research of a cardiologist, Dr. Randolph Byrd, who has dramatically illustrated the healing power of prayer. He has shown that patients whose names were assigned to prayer groups and received daily prayers were 5 times less likely to need antibiotics, 2 1/2 times less likely to experience congestive heart failure, and far less likely to suffer cardiac arrest than those who received no prayers.

Reviewing the messages that fill the pages of Helen Steiner Rice's poetry books in the light of current scientific and spiritual thought tempts one to suggest that Helen had anticipated this new way of looking at our lives by several decades. It would be a mistake to be lured by that temptation. Helen made it quite clear that nothing she advocated in her poems was new. In fact it was ancient advice, culled from the Bible.

The Bible was Helen's constant companion, and she found it to be an indispensable source of whatever wisdom readers found in her poems. For example, the Gospel of Matthew gives great insight into the way the healing of the soul works. It describes the cure of two blind men who followed Jesus crying out, "Son of David, have pity on us!" Jesus spoke to them and asked, "Do you believe that I can do this?" They both said yes, and Jesus touched their eyes saying, "Let it be done for you according to your faith." Both men regained their sight, and although Jesus admonished them to tell no one, the word of his ability to heal spread throughout the land. Matthew's story reveals two important components in the healing process. First, the two men wanted to be healed; they sought the healing touch of Jesus and were open to receiving a change in their lives. Second, they expressed faith in the power of Jesus to give them sight. Only then did the touch of Jesus heal them.

Those who find healing through the message of Helen Steiner Rice, a message that derives entirely from her own faith in God, are similar to the men in the Scripture story. In every case they are people whose lives have been plunged into chaos by events they did not anticipate and could not control. They have struggled unsuccessfully to sort out events on their own. They have searched for an answer that could ease their pain and confusion. They are receptive to a new explanation or a new attitude. They are ready to have their eyes and hearts opened.

Invariably in the course of this search these people came into contact with a verse or verses of Helen Steiner Rice. To use a different scriptural metaphor, one could say that the seed of Helen's message fell on fertile ground and took root there. Helen assessed her role as that of a channel for God's love and grace. She served as an intermediary to those who were opening their lives to God in a fuller way.

Helen's healing words touched crippling attitudes such as self-hate, bitterness, and anger, and while troubles did not disappear from the lives of those who loved her poetry, they took on a different aspect—people grew more peaceful, more accepting, more compassionate as a result of their encounters with Helen Steiner Rice. And so her readers grew in numbers creating what Helen herself described as a "human chain of love around the world."

Gloria Brooks, who even as a child felt the power of Helen's words, is a part of that human chain of love. Hers is one of many stories of the healing power of Helen Steiner Rice. Through her faith in God and Helen's guidance, Gloria has become a "wounded healer."

The Story of Gloria

Gloria Burke Brooks was a little girl when she first met Helen at Wesley Chapel in downtown Cincinnati. "I remember her giving her testimony and how much it meant to me personally as a young person," Gloria recalls. "I loved the woman." Helen Steiner Rice brought healing and transformation into Gloria Brooks's life in more ways than one. "I was a person who needed to know God loved me," Gloria says, adding that while she felt love very strongly from her mother, she did not feel it from her father. "Hearing Mrs. Rice give her testimony enabled my faith to grow," she explains. It was among the people of her church, where Helen was a prominent member of the congregation, that Gloria felt loved. There she struggled with the important decision of her vocation in life and there felt supported to become what God wanted her to be, an ordained Methodist minister. She attended the seminary on a scholarship established at Wesley Chapel by Helen Steiner Rice and put the faith that Helen inspired into action.

Now when Rev. Gloria Brooks gives a devotional workshop for women called the "Beautiful Garden of Prayer," she opens each section with a poem by Helen Steiner Rice. Participants of all ages respond enthusiastically to the poetry. "It really speaks to them," Gloria says. "It is so down to earth, so clear. It touches the heart; it touches you where you are."

No matter how strong our Christian commitment, Gloria suggests, we still need to be reminded at life's difficult times of God's continuous presence. She found herself desperately needing such a reminder in 1987. Her appendix ruptured but somehow closed itself off again. During the next four months symptoms caused by its periodic leakage went undiagnosed despite the best efforts of her physicians. Nevertheless, she would regularly get violently ill. On one occasion she was even hospitalized, but the symptoms disappeared and all tests came back normal. That pattern repeated itself until one day she finally returned to the emergency room near death. A CAT scan followed, then emergency exploratory surgery. The unusually ruptured appendix was finally diagnosed, but all the while Gloria Brooks lay critically ill.

At that juncture the words of Helen Steiner Rice again provided much needed inspiration and encouragement to help Gloria recover fully. "My aunt sent me a Helen Steiner Rice poetry book at that time," Gloria recalls. "The poems had spoken to her and she knew they would also speak to me." Lying desperately ill in her hospital bed, Gloria read the book over and over as the healing process began. She believes that Helen Steiner Rice brought something extra to her struggle for survival, something that the medical profession could not contribute. Gloria healed, and as she did, her faith grew stronger.

Today Rev. Brooks not only uses Helen's poems in her retreats for women, but she also gives Helen Steiner Rice's poetry to the high school seniors in her congregation. The book she gives the most is *Daily Pathways,* because the graduates are entering new pathways of life. "It is a gift that will help them in their faith," she says. She also continues to draw on the wisdom of Helen's poetry herself. "When I read her poetry, I feel her heart there."

In the 1960s and 1970s letters poured in to Helen from people who suffered terribly from loss, adversity, loneliness, depression, disability, and infirmity. Those who wrote had no idea how

Helen managed to capture so perfectly in rhymed verses the pain they struggled to overcome or how she found the exact words to comfort and heal them. The answer was simple. Helen was able to understand and then put into words the suffering of others because she had suffered so much herself.

"Part of her work," says Gloria Brooks, "was a healing of herself." Helen lived and wrote as a wounded healer. In that capacity she charted pathways to healing. Her poems and letters give readers a spiritual map to follow, one they can trust because she traversed it herself on her own life journey.

The people who say they have been changed by the poetry of Helen Steiner Rice are ordinary people who collectively have encountered all of life's many difficulties. Some are sick, others lonely; some have lost their dreams, others their loved ones. Still others feel misunderstood, isolated, or rejected. Taken together, their problems are a catalogue of the bleaker side of life in the closing years of the twentieth century. Yet they all have one thing in common, a quest for healing.

Sooner or later their search required each one of them to have faith, and Helen Steiner Rice's words gave readers the strength to find that faith. Her poems and correspondence lead us through faith to wholeness—if we choose to be touched by the healer, if we choose to transform the heartaches of our lives.

Helen's Pattern for Healing

1. Binding wounds.

Ask yourself: Can I believe that life is a teacher? Can I learn something of value from every event and every person in my life, no matter how painful the encounter? Can I treat myself with love but avoid self-pity?

2. Accepting what is in faith.

Ask yourself: Am I willing to live the faith I profess? Can I trust that my life is unfolding according to God's plan for me, whether or not I like what is happening? Can I move beyond my personal distress and surrender my will to God?

3. Choosing to heal.

Ask yourself: Can I transcend the attitude of the victim? Can I choose to heal my spirit? Can I grow in compassion as I face my own life hurts and forgive my own mistakes? Can I then be a companion to others as they struggle to forgive and heal themselves?

Two

Healing the Pain of Loss

God never hurts us needlessly
And never wastes our pain
For every loss that's sent to us
Is followed by rich gain.

ow hard it is to understand those lines by Helen Steiner Rice when we are first overwhelmed by our losses! Each loss seems unique, and every one hurts so much. Yet no matter how hard we try to prevent pain, life requires all of us to face the pain of losing something—our loved ones, our possessions, and even our dreams. Some losses, such as the death of a child, a spouse, a parent, or a friend, take away those we cherish and make us feel that nothing can fill the void. Others—the loss of a job, for example—rob us of our sense of security and having some meaningful role in the greater scheme of things. Different kinds of losses, like acts of betrayal or events that shatter our dreams, strip us of our self-esteem. Whatever form our losses take, one thing is certain: They force us to change.

No one knew this better than Helen. One reason her words have struck such a responsive chord in those who grieve is that she was well acquainted with loss herself. As someone who had suffered catastrophic loss and understood its hurt all too well, she quickly came to realize that the way we interpret loss determines whether the changes it forces on us are life-giving or self-destructive. The key to transcending loss for Helen was her ability to interpret it symbolically. She came to view loss not merely as an end, but also as a period of transition that precedes new growth.

One of Helen's greatest strengths is that she identified with the heartache that arose from her readers' losses. Yes, she affirmed, loss is difficult; yes, it is painful; yes, we must grieve before we can move on. But at the same time she sent a clear message to her readers: If we have faith, loss can be accepted as part of the mystery of God's higher plan, and armed with that knowledge we can transform our loss into a source of strength for ourselves and others. She assured her readers that the moment of greatest heartache would pass, and she encouraged them to look beyond their own pain. Once they could do that, she promised a divine perspective would unfold in their lives. When the true message of hope takes root in the heart of anyone who has suffered a loss, then and only then healing can begin.

Helen's poetry, along with letters she wrote to those who struggled with loss, leave no doubt that she envisioned healing from loss as a process that included three stages: grieving the loss; accepting it; and finally, transforming it into something beneficial. This chapter opens with the story of Kathy, a woman who credits Helen Steiner Rice's poetry with guiding her through all three of these stages.

The Story of Kathy

The tear stains remain on the worn, loose-leaf note-book pages of the letter that introduced Kathy Klein-holtz to Helen Steiner Rice. Kathy treasures those pages as a precious memory of her infant daughter—"They are all I have left of her," she says—and a reminder of how much Helen's poems have comforted her over the years. Kathy and her husband had so anticipated the birth of their first child, but when that baby arrived in February 1987, something was terribly wrong. Kathy's daughter was born with most of her brain missing. The baby for whom they had waited so long lived for only two days. Kathy was left with an empty nursery and a broken heart she thought could never be mended.

Kathy's cousin Debbie, who had read and loved the poetry of Helen Steiner Rice for years, wrote Kathy a letter and included in it some poems she thought might help Kathy through her pain. "I'm not real good at expressing my thoughts in words," wrote Debbie, "but I'm a very big fan of Helen Steiner Rice. So I have chosen a few writings of hers that I hope will give you something maybe a little uplifting to hold on to."

Right before Debbie's letter arrived in the mail, Kathy dreamed that a lady came to her and told her that everything would be all right. Kathy awoke from that dream certain that she could endure the grief, that her baby was with God, and that it would not be long before she would have other, healthy children. Then Debbie's letter was delivered. It contained three poems: "There Is a Reason for Everything," "Life's Bitterest Disappointments Are God's Sweetest Appointments," and "Your

Problems! My Problems! Our Problems!" Every word of those Helen Steiner Rice poems seemed to echo the encouraging message Kathy had received from the lady in her dream.

As it turned out, Debbie was right to follow her instincts in sending the letter to her grieving cousin. The messages in those poems touched Kathy so profoundly that she asked the priest who presided at her baby's graveside service to read two of them. Afterward she distributed copies of the verses to those in attendance.

During the weeks and months after her daughter's funeral, Kathy frequently woke up in the middle of the night, picked up Debbie's letter and the poems, and reread the wise, heartfelt words of Helen Steiner Rice. "I read them so many times when all I wanted to do was cry, and I felt so much better," Kathy remembers. "Every single word had meaning."

The poem "There Is a Reason for Everything" has special significance to Kathy. "If you read it, it tells you that every loss God sends to us is followed by rich gain. That is exactly how it happened for me down the road," she recalls. "I had a son thirteen months later and sixteen months after that I had another daughter, and they're both fine. It's all right there. If you listen and read what she wrote, it's all there."

Kathy believes Helen Steiner Rice must have been very close to God to be able to write the way she did. "She would have been a wonderful minister," Kathy says with an appreciative smile, "and in a way she was." Helen's poems helped Kathy draw more deeply on her own faith to look for meaning and purpose in the death of her daughter. They also strengthened Kathy to face life's challenges with confidence and sharpened her awareness of all the many gifts she had received.

Kathy now uses the poems that guided her through her grief and healing in her continuing efforts to comfort others who have lost children. One night while she was working at the switchboard of a local hospital, a new mother whose baby had

There Is a Reason for Everything

Our Father knows what's best for us,
So why should we complain—
We always want the sunshine,
But He knows there must be rain—
We love the sound of laughter
And the merriment of cheer,
But our hearts would lose their tenderness
If we never shed a tear.
Our Father tests us often
With suffering and with sorrow,
He tests us, not to punish us,
But to help us meet tomorrow . . .
For growing trees are strengthened
When they withstand the storm,
And the sharp cut of the chisel
Gives the marble grace and form . . .
God never hurts us needlessly,
And He never wastes our pain,
For every loss He sends to us
Is followed by rich gain . . .
And when we count the blessings
That God has so freely sent
We will find no cause for murmuring
And no time to lament.
For our Father loves His children
And to Him all things are plain,
So He never sends us pleasures
When the soul's deep need is pain . . .
So whenever we are troubled
And when everything goes wrong,
It is just God working in us
To make our spirit strong.

just died called several times because she needed assistance in dialing. When Kathy expressed her sympathy, the young mother revealed that her baby had suffered from anencephalitis—the same disorder that had taken the life of Kathy's daughter. Naturally Kathy understood the woman's pain, so she reached out. After sharing her own story, Kathy explained how Helen Steiner Rice's poems had seen her through her darkest days. She immediately sent copies of Helen's poems to the grieving mother.

In transforming her own loss Kathy Kleinholtz has become another link in Helen Steiner Rice's human chain of love and she continues her good work. When a neighbor died, Kathy sent his widow one of Helen's poems. A short time later, when Kathy learned that her own mother was diagnosed with colon cancer, she resolved to send her poems by Helen every week. Kathy was certain that they would not just make her mother feel better, but they would also encourage her to fight the disease. The poems make a lot of sense, says Kathy; they mean so much because they are true. Kathy expresses her feelings about Helen simply and poignantly: "If you can look at things like she did, it brings you comfort. Her poems make you feel better so you want to make other people feel better."

To Helen the Easter story of the resurrection expressed most eloquently the truth about all loss, even death. Many years after her husband's suicide, she explained to a friend that she had reached her conclusions about death, loss, and resurrection when she reflected on how her life had been shaped after losing her husband. In a very revealing letter, she wrote:

> You know, it is so true that if we just wait and keep on trusting God even when hope is gone, He will turn the greatest disappointment into a compensation and the deepest sorrow into joy, for the joy of Easter was born of the sorrow of Good Friday.

40

Loss according to Helen was only one piece in an eternal cycle of life, death, and rebirth. She recalled it most effectively when she drew on the basic message of the Easter story to write a comforting letter to a woman whose son was dying:

> On Good Friday, that mother could not see beyond her grief, or envision the glory of Easter Sunday and know that her sorrow would be turned to rejoicing. And neither can you see beyond this present minute of suffering, anxiety and uncertainty. . . . This is your Good Friday, and it will lead you to a day of *rejoicing*— sometime, somewhere and somehow.

Helen Steiner Rice intuitively realized that if she viewed loss not as an end, but as part of a process that gave rise to new life and growth, then she did not simply have to endure it; she could learn from its pain and suffering, heal, and go forward.

Helen was able to observe in her own life the truth inherent in the pattern demonstrated by the resurrection story. What is more important, she was able to express it in a way everyone can understand. The loss of her father was devastating but it prompted her to grow in maturity and self-sufficiency. Helen's opportunity to attend college and law school was irretrievably lost, but she nevertheless taught herself how to be a successful saleswoman and public relations officer who, as a popular speaker, urged business leaders to recognize the talents of women. In other words, she turned experiences that might have made her bitter and resentful into lessons that both saved her and inspired others. Helen believed that her talent for helping others through her poetry resulted directly from what she learned in the aftermath of personal tragedy.

What she had learned from her own life Helen Steiner Rice eagerly shared with others. Her correspondence leaves no doubt that her letters, just like her poetry, urged those who wrote her to look for the deeper meaning of loss and to deal with it in a healthy and positive way. Her letters to Margaret, a woman she never met, make it clear how necessary it is to grieve loss openly. They also offer a perfect blueprint for accepting loss as part of the mystery of God's higher plan and transforming it into a source of healing and renewal.

The Story of Margaret

Helen heard from a mutual friend about the death of Margaret's son Jay, an eighteen-year-old high school student who died from severe burns on the upper part of his body. She sent Margaret a book of inspirational poetry, and that expression of sympathy encouraged Margaret to respond. In a letter to Helen, Margaret fondly recalled all of her son's many wonderful qualities. He had been captain of the wrestling team and a district wrestling champion. He was also intrigued by the beauty of nature and loved children, especially his nieces. "He was never too busy to pick one or both of them up after school and play with or make over them," wrote Margaret. In fact Jay had taken three little neighbor boys on a camping trip just one week before the fire. Along with his wonderful relationship with children, he also worked hard on the family farm and even harder on his studies. "He was a special boy, and I think that is why God wanted him," wrote the grieving mother. "No one knows the lonesomeness we feel not having him here."

Helen acknowledged to Margaret that she understood how hard it was to pass through the time of acute grieving. "I know it is difficult for you to dry your tears and stop the 'heart-hurt' that you constantly feel," she wrote. Helen echoed Margaret's bewilderment at the sudden death of this healthy young person who had so much promise: "It is hard to reconcile ourselves to such a loss when God asks us to give up someone young and in mid-career with abundant years stretching ahead of them, for to have a life so suddenly silenced is beyond our understanding."

But Helen also reassured Margaret that a time would come when the pain of the loss would diminish: "I know there is nothing much that I can say to soften your sorrow right now. But, in time, you will be able to push it back into the haven of your heart and go on, meeting each day as it comes." In a subsequent letter Helen explained to Margaret how in time she and her husband might accept the loss of their son as part of a divine plan, for his death had "opened spiritual doors" in all their hearts.

> When you look back across your lives, you will see that he, in his wonderful, unselfish loving way, made you all aware of what life is all about, for he gave generously of his love. And his love changed the lives of the young and the old, of family and friends. . . . . What more could parents ask? So take this gift from God, and, in accepting it, do all things just as you think he would like you to do them.

Margaret's letter in response to Helen's reassuring words leaves no doubt that Helen's poems had been a great source of comfort to her. Like Helen, Margaret was a faith-filled woman. "I'm surely glad we have faith in God or nothing would seem worthwhile anymore," wrote Margaret to Helen. The grieving mother's own deep faith allowed her to open up to Helen's healing message.

Helen urged Margaret to continue to lean on God for comfort but she also urged her to recognize that new insights were being born in her through the experience of this loss. "You are now privileged to share your understanding and love with others who need your compassion," Helen gently underscored in a responding letter. She encouraged Margaret to think about the possibility that through faith her own suffering could be transformed. "God does not comfort us to make us more comfortable," she wrote; "God comforts us so that we may also become comforters."

Helen Steiner Rice did not confine her assistance to friends who faced losses through death. She knew that loss takes many shapes, but the process of grieving remains a constant. Consequently the same recommendations she made to Margaret that helped her through grieving, accepting, and transforming loss after a death can be seen in her letters to Gordon and to Henry, even though their experiences were quite different.

The Story of Gordon

Helen wrote to Gordon after he was fired without warning during a company restructuring. The loss of his job was compounded, he explained in a letter, because executives at his firm circulated the story that he was leaving because he was "a cold, unfriendly individual who was impossible to get close to and know." Gordon was shocked at this revelation. He had always been happy in his work, was never given reason to think he performed below expectations, and felt he got along well with his colleagues. After much soul-searching and careful examination of the records, Gordon concluded that he was fired because he honestly answered an evaluation form, criticizing some administrative procedures.

Helen contacted Gordon shortly after he lost his job and sympathized with his feelings of shock and dismay. "There are some things that no words have ever been invented to fit, and this is one of them!" she wrote. She realized his loss was especially painful because he had worked so long and faithfully for his company: "What is happening here is only typical of what is happening everywhere in this mad, crazy, confused world, only I think it hurts so much more when it happens to the thing we have cherished and nurtured and believed in for so many years."

Helen cautioned Gordon not to become embittered by his loss as he worked through the problems of accepting it, and

she reinforced in him a sense of his own admirable charac-
teristics. "You have always epitomized honor and integrity and
loyalty," she wrote; "I know that wherever you go or whatever
you undertake, you will succeed, for you have the inherent
qualities that make for success."

Finally, Helen reminded Gordon that he should rely on his
faith when he felt that things would never get better, for only
then could he be transformed by his loss. "Remember that He
who sees above the skyline often comforts us, not by chang-
ing the circumstances of our lives, but our attitude toward
them," she wrote. Gordon responded to Helen's letter grate-
fully and acknowledged that although he was still stunned by
the loss, he was willing to place its outcome in God's hands:
"I still can't believe my work is finished here, but I, too, believe
we are all divinely guided and that some new position will
open up for me."

The Story of Henry

Helen, a longtime resident of the Gibson
Hotel in the heart of downtown Cincinnati,
met Henry Kadetz when he worked for the
hotel as sales manager, convention coordi-
nator, and public relations director. Henry
was a talented singer and entertainer, and
Helen knew he longed to star in major stage
productions. She also knew that Henry's
dream had never come true. Nevertheless,
to Helen, Henry epitomized the lines of her
poem "Climb 'Til Your Dream Comes True."

> Faith is a force that is greater
> Than knowledge or power or skill
> And many defeats turn to triumph
> If you trust in God's wisdom and will.

45

Helen had many opportunities to observe Henry at his job, and she took careful note of his gentleness, his sensitivity, and his eagerness to please the people he served. It was clear to her that on the stage of life Henry was an outstanding performer. When the Gibson Hotel closed in 1974, Henry took a new job. Helen Steiner Rice wrote to wish him well and describe what she called a "little miracle." She wanted Henry to know that, although he had lost his dream of being a top performer, from her point of view he had won center stage in the lives of others.

> You have contributed SO MUCH to SO MANY PEOPLE by being so interested and so helpful to them in arranging their special-occasion dinners, which are always so deeply meaningful to families. . . . They will remember your kindness to them long after the stage celebrities are forgotten.

Helen congratulated Henry on being a real star in the hearts of the people he served and urged him to continue in the role of making people happy. He followed her advice. Over the years Henry gave his time and talent to helping others find employment and played a key part in the renovation and expansion of a local senior citizens' center. Henry died in September 1996. His wife found among his treasures the decades-old letter from Helen Steiner Rice congratulating him on transforming his cherished dream.

"Nothing on Earth Is Forever Yours," wrote Helen, except for the love of God. Yet she knew how hard it was to let go of loved ones, of careers, of dreams, and sometimes even of the way we look at life. She always stood by her friends through their losses, often helping them to see more clearly that loss is not always an enemy to be feared. "Remember, many good things are born when things look bad," she encouraged a young man who had suffered a terrible blow to his self-esteem. She reas-

Nothing on Earth Is Forever Yours— Only the Love of the Lord Endures!

Everything in life is passing
And whatever we possess
Cannot endure forever
But ends in nothingness,
For there are no safety boxes
Nor vaults that can contain
The possessions we collected
And desire to retain . . .
So all that we acquire,
Be it power, fame or jewels
Is but limited and earthly,
Only "treasure made for fools" . . .
For only in God's Kingdom
Can we find enduring treasure,
Priceless gifts of love and beauty—
More than we can ever measure,
And these become the "riches"
We can keep and part with never,
For only in God's Kingdom
Do our treasures last forever . . .
So use the word forever
With sanctity and love,
For nothing is forever
But the love of God above!

sured him that his loss was not the end of the world; it was simply God's signal that he should be making a change in his life.

In many letters of sympathy Helen reminded those who suffered the loss of a loved one that we do not always have to think of death as terrible in its finality. Sometimes, she counseled one coworker, death can provide a welcome release: "I know that even in the midst of your sorrow you are aware that God, in His wonderful way, which is beyond all our understanding, has taken your dear mother out of the world of pain that she lived in for the last year." Helen consoled another woman, whose husband had passed away after a period of prolonged suffering, "Death came as a kind friend."

Memories, Helen believed, were particularly valuable tools in transforming loss into something uplifting. For one thing, they contain the precious lessons taught by loved ones when they were alive, lessons that continue to teach us long after their death. Memories also keep loved ones near, Helen wrote in a letter supporting a friend who had lost her mother: "I always think of my beloved mother as having just passed into the next room, beyond the sight of my vision and the touch of my hands, but there are so many memories of her dearness that live in my heart that she is never very far away from me."

The pain and joy of life had taught Helen that memories could convert the negative force of loss into the beneficial energy of change, for memories fuel something that is both painful and creative. When the father of a coworker died, Helen reassured his widow, "The memories of your years together and all that you have experienced in those years will provide strength for you to go on . . . and while memories will make your loss agonizingly keen, those same memories will bring him very close to you."

Helen's letters helped her friends heal and transform their losses much in the same way as her poems do today. In each of the stories that follow, healing from loss began or continued because one of Helen Steiner Rice's poems met an individual's specific need. In the first story the transformation of loss into new growth could not even start until a young mother discovered her lost tears.

The Story of Margie

One October day Margie's child was playing near a railroad track when a train came along. The little boy did not hear the train coming, and when the engineer tried to warn him by blowing the whistle, its cord broke. It was impossible to stop the train, and tragically, the youngster's body was dragged more than a mile down the tracks.

Margie accepted the news of her child's death without crying a tear. The little boy was buried and the accident was never brought up as a topic of discussion in the family. Indeed, no one in the household—not Margie, her husband, or their daughter—ever mentioned the child's name. The loss, unmourned and unhealed, hung silently over their home. Margie could not let herself grieve the death of her son, so neither she nor her family could take the first painful steps that would lead to healing from a heartbreaking loss.

On the tenth anniversary of the little boy's death, Margie went to visit her aunt, who had always appreciated and found solace in Helen Steiner Rice's cards and books. Margie sat at the kitchen table leafing through her aunt's collection of poems and finally came to a group of sympathy cards that triggered a reaction that had lain dormant too long. Suddenly she laid her head down on the table and began to cry uncontrollably.

The aunt wrote to Helen reporting what she called a miracle. "God, through you, has opened the floodgates and all the anguish that has been stored in her heart for ten years was poured out in almost incoherent words and broken sentences," she wrote. When Margie finally regained her composure, she began to talk to her aunt about the loss of her son and how it related to her thoughts about God. Her aunt said:

Margie . . . thanked me for letting her see and read your poems and told me they were the first things that had really touched her since she heard the news of the tragedy! . . . She said she had never resented God taking Donnie, but she just could not give him up until she read your beautiful poems!

When Margie left her aunt that day, she took along the poem "This Too Will Pass Away," which ends with these lines:

> I know God will break "all the chains"
> That are binding me tight in "the darkness"
> And trying to fill me with fear—
> For there is no night without dawning
> And I know that "my morning" is near.

The chains that had bound Margie in silence for so many years had finally been broken; she was free to grieve the death of her son. She parted from her aunt with the words, "I shall pray for Helen Steiner Rice! Tell her that only *her* poems have ever been able to reach my heart. Tell her also that my fountain of tears was dry, or so I thought, until *she* opened the floodgates!"

Helen responded to the aunt's recounting of this episode in a letter written on the anniversary of Franklin Rice's suicide. Helen wrote that in grieving Franklin's death she had somehow managed to learn how to help others grieve. "I recognize it is tragedy that illuminates our lives and all sorrow is a stepping stone to a richer, fuller life."

If anyone needed Helen's help in grieving the loss of her child, Margie certainly did. She could neither accept nor transform that calamity until Helen Steiner Rice made it possible for her to give voice to her feelings. Margie teaches us that every step in the process of transforming loss is a crucial one. In the following story that lesson is even clearer. Although Karen can identify her feelings, she nevertheless struggles to accept and transform the experience of her loss.

The Story of Karen

Karen Christopfel's son Jake was born in February 1996 with a cleft palate and missing most of his brain. Karen knew even before Jake was born that he faced a short and tortured life. She and her husband brought him home to his sister and two brothers determined to fill whatever time he had with love and support. For nearly three months Karen painstakingly fed Jake through a tube doctors had inserted in his throat. At the same time a registered nurse administered medications that would control the inevitable violent seizures accompanying his condition. At first Jake defied every medical prediction. Instead of giving up he gained weight and grew. In May, however, when he was only eighty-one days old, Jake died.

When Karen's niece had suffered complications from surgery two years before Jake's birth, Karen had sent the child's mother, her sister, Helen Steiner Rice's poem "There Is a Reason for Everything." Now Karen found herself seeking the answer to her own tearful why? from reading the same poem. Another of Helen's poems brought Karen greater comfort, however. On the day following Jake's death Karen received a copy of the poem "All Nature Tells Us Nothing Really Ever Dies." It starts with these lines:

> Nothing really ever dies
> That is not born anew—
> The miracles of nature
> All tell us this is true.

All Nature Tells Us Nothing Really Ever Dies

Nothing really ever dies
That is not born anew—
The miracles of nature
All tell us this is true . . .
The flowers sleeping peacefully
Beneath the winter's snow
Awaken from their icy grave
When Spring winds start to blow
And little brooks and singing streams,
Icebound beneath the snow,
Begin to babble merrily
Beneath the sun's warm glow . . .
And all around on every side
New life and joy appear
To tell us nothing ever dies
And we should have no fear,
For death is just a detour
Along life's wending way
That leads God's chosen children
To a bright and glorious day.

"I knew when Jake died he went to heaven," Karen recalls, "but when I read this I just *felt* it, *felt* it in my heart. And he died in May, which was the springtime, and this poem tells us in the springtime life begins again."

Helen Steiner Rice's poems have continued to sustain Karen throughout the process of grieving and are especially helpful as she faces what she understands is her anger toward God. "When you go through grief, you get angry at God," she says. "You ask, 'Why?' Helen Steiner Rice's poems bring you closer to God. You realize God is your source of comfort and you have to turn to him." When Karen struggles with the question of why Jake died, she returns to the poem "There Is a Reason for Everything." Every time she reads the line that assures her every loss in life is followed by rich gain, she remembers all the ways Jake enriched her life.

One of the lessons Karen learned through the experience was that when things seemed to be worse than anyone could imagine, she could always pray and seek God's help. God is always there. Karen also learned that she is never alone. During the darkest days she found support from her family, her friends, and her church. It meant so much just to have someone sit and talk with her. Karen now sees this devastating experience as one that has helped her learn to respect and honor all life in a deeper way. Jake may have been blind and deaf, but Karen was sure that he responded to her loving presence. As a result she has learned to count her blessings, among them her three healthy children. Her experience has led her to deeper compassion for others. As she puts it, "Everyone has a story to tell, and no matter how bad you have it, somebody else has it worse."

Karen has no doubt that Helen Steiner Rice's poems bring people closer to God. Her son Jake was born on Valentine's Day, and she will always find special consolation in Helen's poem "The Legend of the Valentine." The first lines of the verse "The legend says St. Valentine / was in a prison cell" are especially meaningful for Karen, for she understands them in the context of her lost son. "That was Jake," Karen says, drawing the parallel between St. Valentine and her son. "He was trapped inside his body." The poem ends with lines that summarize for Karen the experience of caring for her Jake:

> Faith and Love can triumph,
> No matter where you are,
> For Faith and Love are Greater
> Than the strongest prison bar.

When she reflects on all that has occurred in her life, Karen comes back to those lines. "It's true," she says. "Jake was God's gift of love to us. Love is what he was."

Like Margie and Karen, Barbara too lost a child. Her story is one about learning when the time has come to move beyond grief.

The Story of Barbara

Barbara's daughter, Debbie, was twenty-three years old when she was struck and killed by a drunk driver. "She was the greatest daughter anyone could ask for," Barbara recalls, "always laughing, cheering people up, and caring so much for others." Her daughter's death was the worst thing that ever happened to Barbara, but one night shortly after the accident, she dreamed that Debbie was standing close by saying, "Don't cry—it's time to stop." It was a vivid dream. Barbara could see a book with yellow flowers on the cover, and inside the book was a poem that repeated her daughter's message. Shortly thereafter Barbara went to a neighborhood bookstore, and one of the first items she saw was a Helen Steiner Rice poetry book with yellow flowers on the cover. Inside was a poem of consolation. Naturally Barbara wanted to buy the book but much to her chagrin she discovered that she didn't have the money.

When I Must Leave You

When I must leave you for a little while,
Please do not grieve and shed wild tears
And hug your sorrow to you through the years,
But start out bravely with a gallant smile;
And for my sake and in my name,
Live on and do all things the same.
Feed not your loneliness on empty days,
But fill each waking hour in useful ways.
Reach out your hand in comfort and in cheer,
And I, in turn, will comfort you and hold you near.
And never, never be afraid to die,
For I am waiting for you in the sky.

Unfortunately, when she went back to the store a few days later, the book was gone. She searched for it for years.

Helen's book *Loving Promises* features a cover with yellow, white, and purple flowers. Inside on a page illustrated with yellow and white daffodils is the poem "When I Must Leave You." Helen wrote it to commemorate the death of her mother, and it carries a message remarkably similar to the one Debbie outlined to her mother in the dream:

> When I must leave you for a little while,
> Please do not grieve and shed wild tears
> And hug your sorrow to you through the years,
> But start out bravely with a gallant smile;
> And for my sake and in my name,
> Live on and do all things the same.

Barbara realized that Debbie did not want her to keep crying, so she found a way to transform her pain into thankfulness and forgiveness. Now Barbara frequently reflects on how grateful she is that God let her have Debbie for twenty-three years and she also thinks about the man who killed her daughter. "I don't hate the drunk driver that killed her," she writes. "I don't know what he has to go through either; maybe it eats away at him. I pray for him and I understand he belongs to AA now and that he's helping others."

Barbara's experience has made her an ardent fan of Helen Steiner Rice's poetry, so much so that she describes Helen as a "blessing from God."

Barbara's willingness to look with compassion on the man who killed her daughter, like Karen's struggle with her anger toward God over the loss of her son, teaches us that forgiveness is an important part of accepting and transforming a loss.

We can see this truth in the story of Stella, who, as a young woman, lost her reputation and her self-esteem. Years later she found healing through the power of forgiveness and the help of Helen Steiner Rice.

The Story of Stella

Stella loved The Salvation Army and eagerly looked forward to turning eighteen, the minimum age when she could sign up for missionary work in another city. Full of energy and eager to advance God's message of love, Stella completely trusted the army officers at the mission to which she was assigned. Not long after her arrival there, however, Stella's life changed forever.

She and two other young women had been given rooms in the house of one of the officers. She was delighted, especially because the housing arrangements offered the opportunity to play with the family's young daughters. It seemed like paradise to Stella, but she was quickly brought down to earth. One night when no one else was at home, the officer sexually assaulted her. Stella tearfully reported the incident to the local hierarchy of the church. The next thing she knew, three female officers were cross-examining her, and one slapped her until she was bruised. They told her the good name of an entire family would be ruined because of her charge.

The women denounced Stella, claiming she had made up the entire story. Confused and feeling obligated to choose between loyalty to herself and her devotion to the two young daughters of her attacker, Stella elected to withdraw her accusation. Instantly branded as a liar, she fled from the mission to which she had devoted herself. She spent many years unsuccessfully trying to reconcile herself with her faith, but she could not forgive those who betrayed her and, as a result, she could not love or value herself. Stella carried her unhealed losses through much of her life.

Many years later Stella described her state of mind in a letter to Helen Steiner Rice.

Even when I prayed I could not speak about it to God, and when I came to the line, "Forgive us our trespasses *as we forgive,*" I could go no farther. My soul was filled with bitterness, my heart with hatred; hatred of three persons—BITTER HATRED! And worse— I thought I was justified. They had lied about me and caused me to "run away."

Then Stella read Helen's poem "Two Palestinian Seas," which compares the Sea of Galilee to the Dead Sea.

> One is a sparkling sapphire jewel,
> Its waters are clean and clear and cool . . .
> One of the seas, like liquid sun
> Can warm the hearts of everyone,
> While farther south another sea
> Is dead and dark and miserly . . .
> It hoards and holds the Jordan's waves
> Until like shackled, captured slaves
> The fresh, clear Jordan turns to salt
> And dies within the Dead Sea's vault . . .

Stella decided that she had lived much of her life as the Dead Sea. She wept bitterly over her years of estrangement from the church she had loved; then she wrote to one of the women she had resented for so long—the other two had died. When Stella finished that task, she prayed for forgiveness. The transformation she experienced within herself was nothing short of miraculous. "It seems to me God wrought a miracle in my life too—through you," she wrote to Helen. "You have rekindled my self-respect."

In her response to Stella, Helen urged her to put the losses of the past behind her. "You definitely are not the Dead Sea!" she encouraged. "With God," she continued, "nobody is ever a loser. . . . And you can walk with a happy heart, secure in the knowledge that in God's eyes you are truly a bright star!"

It takes time—months, years, or even decades—to move through the cycle of healing from loss to rebirth in the way that Helen Steiner Rice outlines in her poems and letters. Our losses differ; some are more devastating than others, but each is uniquely our own. How deeply we are affected by loss also depends on our individual personality and life situation. Helen understood all of this. She also understood that healing from any kind of loss is made easier if one has faith in God.

Helen Steiner Rice was a woman of great faith, and faith is the ingredient common to every person included in this chapter's stories about healing life's losses. Helen realized that faith in God makes it possible not only for people to grasp the symbolic meaning of the Easter story, but also to believe that life's losses will somehow be transformed. Helen knew her poems and letters were not answers in themselves; they simply pointed the way. Those who truly want to turn every loss into rich gain must live in faith. Then the resurrection cycle of life, death, and rebirth will complete itself for them.

Helen's Pattern for Healing the Pain of Loss

1. Facing and grieving the loss.

Ask yourself: Have I really allowed myself to experience my pain? Can I acknowledge the dimensions of my loss? Can I let myself cry, question, be angry, share the hurt with others, and feel overwhelmed for a period? Can I express my pain without shame?

2. Accepting that loss is part of life.

Ask yourself: Can I accept that loss is inevitable and comes to all of us? Can I accept my loss as part of God's plan, even though it may lead me in directions that contradict my plans for the future? Can I reassure myself that this loss can be part of a time of rebirth for me?

3. Transforming the loss.

Ask yourself: Can I understand my loss as part of an eternal cycle of life, death, and rebirth? Can I derive something from my loss that will help me become wiser and more compassionate? Can I choose to renew life and make my loss a source of enrichment?

Three

Healing the Pain
of Adversity

The way we use adversity
Is strictly our own choice
For in God's hands adversity
Can make the heart rejoice.

hen we receive bad news, rejoicing is the furthest thing from our mind. Typically we say to ourselves, *Why me? What else can go wrong? Can this really be happening?* Sometimes our own errors open the door to adversity and we reap the consequences of our mistakes. Often, however, heartache comes like the strike of a bolt of lightning, with no warning and no time to prepare. When we face financial disaster, or our doctor discovers cancer, or our child is diagnosed with an incurable disease, then we are suddenly confronted with adversity in its raw, unvarnished form.

If we can check the impulse to focus on ourselves and instead pause to look around us, we will quickly realize that we are not alone in our suffering. Everyone faces adversity. No one escapes the problems of life; they arrive, often unbidden and always unwelcome. But they are guests we cannot turn away. And unexpected troubles, like surprise visitors, test our responses. Will we receive them grudgingly or graciously? In her poems and letters to those who suffered adversity, Helen Steiner Rice made her position perfectly clear: Our troubles can become our greatest teachers. She suggested that adversity, like loss, could be viewed symbolically. Look at adversity not as a punishment, but as a way of growing in wisdom, Helen advised. Look beyond the problem; ask what it is teaching you about life.

Helen offered hope that something good can come from even the worst experience if you reflect on certain specific realities. First, remember that trouble is a part of everyone's life, so your difficulties are not unique. Second, do not waste your time with the futile lament, Why me? It is far better to surrender your troubles to God and pray for guidance. Finally, let adversity help you develop as a human being. If you give them the chance, your heartaches can make you wiser and more compassionate. That is the theme of this chapter, which opens with the story of Etta. Sustained by the wisdom of Helen's poetry, Etta used her own adversity to create a more caring world for children with cancer.

The Story of Etta

Etta Hoeh stood in her doctor's office in the autumn of 1972 and wept. Her eleven-year-old son, Jeffrey—positive, caring, outgoing Jeffrey—had just been diagnosed with Hodgkin's disease. She was grief-stricken and overwhelmed. How could she juggle his chemotherapy and radiation treatments with her job and her other seven children, half of whom were still in grade school? "Who ever promised you a rose garden?" asked the doctor. His comment left Etta stunned and angry. She needed support and comfort, and what she got from the doctor sounded like an unfeeling platitude. All the way home, however, she reflected on his words.

Disturbed though she was, Etta knew from long years of experience that there was at least one source of comfort she could rely on. As a young woman she had clipped and saved poems by Helen Steiner Rice whenever they appeared in the newspaper. She always found them inexplicably helpful and uplifting. One poem stood out, "Let Not Your Heart Be Troubled." It was Etta's favorite. She had fallen in love with the verses the first time she saw them displayed at the home of her husband's aunt. Now the poem sat, a gift from the aunt, in a worn white frame on Etta's dresser. It had comforted Etta in times of adversity before because, as she put it, the poem "said it all."

Whenever Etta was troubled she would go to the dresser, pick up the framed poem, study it, read it over carefully, and meditate on its meaning, even though she already knew the words by heart. Perhaps that poem more than anything else helped her deal with her fears for the safety of her husband, a career military officer in an airborne division, when he was sent overseas, first to Korea and later to Vietnam. "It got me through so much," Etta recalls; "I just relied on it so."

Etta always followed the poem's advice systematically, step by step. She took her troubles to God, she reflected on the Gospel story of Christ calming the Sea of Galilee, then she stopped when she came to these lines:

> And then I just keep quiet
> and think only thoughts of peace.

She made herself be very still. "I'd try to be real quiet and just think about it, and think, well, I *can* get through this. This will

63

Let Not Your Heart Be Troubled

Whenever I am troubled
And lost in deep despair
I bundle all my troubles up
And go to God in prayer.
I tell Him I am heartsick
And lost and lonely, too,
That my mind is deeply burdened
And I don't know what to do.
But I know He stilled the tempest
And calmed the angry sea
And I humbly ask if in His love
He'll do the same for me.
And then I just keep quiet
And think only thoughts of peace
And if I abide in stillness
My "restless murmurings" cease.

be okay," she says. That poem had never failed to help Etta feel better. Consequently it seemed natural for her to turn to it once again in 1972, when Jeffrey faced an uncertain future.

Jeffrey, the fifth of Etta's eight children, was repeatedly hospitalized as physicians fought against his illness. First came treatments to force the Hodgkin's disease into remission. Then over the next sixteen years Jeffrey suffered from shingles, Graves' disease, another form of lymphoma, and finally a paralysis that began in his feet and ultimately confined him to a wheelchair.

Over and over, Helen Steiner Rice's words ran through Etta's mind:

> Whenever I am troubled
> and lost in deep despair
> I bundle all my troubles up
> and go to God in prayer.

Etta had a copy of "Let Not Your Heart Be Troubled" framed for Jeffrey, hoping it would encourage him every day. Each time he was hospitalized she set it on his bedside table. Etta believed it comforted Jeffrey during those times when she and her family could not be with him. "I just know that he had to read that at times when we weren't there, and I'm sure it had to help him," she says.

Jeffrey was courageous and maintained his positive outlook even when he was placed in isolation at Cincinnati Children's Hospital in December 1988. Several of his brothers and sisters had strep throat at the time, so they couldn't visit their brother. Etta, dividing her time between the sick children at home and Jeffrey in the hospital, was unable to make her usual preparations for Christmas. Two extraordinary things occurred that December that Etta never forgot. First, a woman whose husband suffered from cancer visited Jeffrey and told him how her family had started a golf tournament to benefit cancer victims. He promised her that when he got better, his family would organize one too. Second, the mother of a little girl in the room next to Jeffrey went home at mid-afternoon on Christmas Day and returned a few hours later, bringing Christmas dinner for Etta and her family. To have a stranger look after her in such a caring way touched Etta deeply.

Although Jeffrey Hoeh's name had been on the bone marrow transplant list at the hospital for some time, his cancer spread before a matching transplant donor could be found. He died in 1989. After Jeffrey passed away, several people sent Etta Hoeh cards that featured Helen Steiner Rice's poem "The End of the Road Is but a Bend in the Road." It helped Etta place her son's death in a tolerable perspective. "When he died, it was like the end of the road," Etta remembers, "but he changed our lives and so I think it became a bend in the road." In the aftermath of his death the Hoeh family set up a memorial fund in Jeffrey's honor to benefit cancer victims. Each year they now sponsor the golf tournament Jeff had promised, and a dance as well. They also spend every Christmas Eve serving dinner at Cincinnati Children's Hospital to families whose children are hospitalized there.

The memorial fund and the joy it brings Etta Hoeh's family became the "bend in the road" that followed Jeffrey's death. "If Helen could only know the lives that she's touched and the ways that she's helped!" Etta exclaims. After Jeffrey died, the Hoeh family planted a beautiful rose garden in the side yard of their family home, and each of Jeff's brothers and sisters placed a memento there. Mrs. Hoeh now smiles with understanding when she recalls the question "Who ever promised you a rose garden?" her doctor asked in 1972. "God gave us a rose garden," says Etta, "just not the one we wanted."

Etta Hoeh has grasped the basic truth of Helen Steiner Rice's understanding of adversity: Troubles are part of everyone's life, and so are moments of desperation. In her poem "Your Problems! My Problems! Our Problems!" Helen points out that trouble not only is a vital part of life, but also, despite at first glance seeming unique to us, is actually experienced by many others.

> Whatever your problem, whatever your cross,
> Whatever your burden, whatever your loss,
> You've got to believe me you are not alone,
> For all of the troubles and trials you have known
> Are faced at this minute by others like you
> Who also cry out, "Oh, God, what shall I do?"

And even though Helen believed that "trouble is life and life is trouble" for everyone, she knew full well that it is only human to wonder why adversity should befall honest, decent people. "We all often wonder *WHY* bad things have to happen to good people," she wrote to her friend Hazel, who was injured in an accident in 1972. "But we all know," Helen continued, "that just being good and loving God and trying to serve him does not guarantee us immunity from trouble, suffering, pain, sickness, and accident."

What then was the point of human suffering? According to Helen the answer to that eternal question was part of the mystery of God's unfathomable wisdom. She believed it was a waste of time and energy to speculate on what caused our misfortunes or to complain about the vagaries of life. She thought it was far preferable and much more profitable to see afflictions as opportunities sent by God. "While it is impossible for us to understand why things happen as they do," Helen wrote in her letter to Hazel, "we must be content to accept everything that comes to us as a gift from God."

Arriving at this perspective did not come easily, Helen acknowledged, but over the years she trained herself to stop trying to figure out why things happened as they did. "I have learned never to question or to try to find the answer," she counseled another friend, "for I know that everything that comes to me in this life is a part of God's plan." That attitude—grounded in the belief that this divine plan teaches us to rely on God—is at the heart of

Helen's gift for helping others. Her poems about relying on God in times of adversity force people to reflect on their own faith. "You always felt there was hope," Etta Hoeh says about reading Helen's poems; "they help you to really think about God, to know there is somebody to help lift us up."

For Helen Steiner Rice healing the pain of adversity meant looking at every problem in life metaphorically. If in fact each misfortune that arose in her life was as she put it "a gift from God," then that divine offering was there to teach her something. The lessons, she explained to Hazel, might not be easily learned, but every one of them confirmed her belief that God never makes mistakes. "There is always a definite purpose behind everything that happens to us (even though we may not always be able to figure out what it is at the time we are experiencing our dark hour)."

Every misfortune, Helen believed, offered an opportunity for spiritual growth and enrichment. Only through the deep experience of suffering was an individual able to understand the pain of others and become compassionate. When afflictions evolved into lessons in self-development, then and only then could the wounds of adversity begin to heal.

Transforming ill fortune into personal growth became a common topic in Helen's correspondence with those who wrote her because they were in agony. Her exchange of letters with Dottie, whose life was thrown into chaos after a diagnosis of cancer, provides a model for how Helen led a friend through the process of accepting her lot in life, understanding it symbolically, and turning it into a mission of carrying love to others.

The Story of Dottie

When Dottie first wrote to Helen Steiner Rice in the autumn of 1967, she was still filled with anger and bitterness, even though a get-well card with one of Helen's poems had already opened the pathway to a new perspective for her. Dottie's world fell apart, she told Helen, when she had extensive surgery for cancer a year earlier. "All I could say was, 'Why me?' over and over again."

At first, Dottie's bitterness was directed toward her husband, largely because she felt he was utterly insensitive to her plight. He rarely spoke about her illness and from her point of view was no help at all. When she was bedridden after the surgery, all the household tasks were simply left undone. "A pig never had to live in the filth I did for the first four months after I came out of the hospital," she reported to Helen. Dottie's frustration quickly grew to fury when she realized that she was helpless to change things: "I was, for the first time in my forty-two years, flat on my back." She lamented to Helen with sincere irony that she had no one to count on, even though she had spent her whole life trying to make others happy while frequently hiding her own sorrow.

When Dottie could finally leave her apartment she began to search for the answer to that self-defeating question, Why me? She thought she might find the answer through organized religion. "I went to every single church within fifteen miles of my town, and, as expected, I could not get the answer," she explained to Helen, adding that she had explored "every religion there is." "You name it and I talked to them all," she said. Then what Dottie described as a "message of truth" appeared in her life. A friend sent her a Helen Steiner Rice poem on a card. She was particularly moved by these lines:

> Our Father tests us often
> With suffering and with sorrow,
> He tests us, not to punish us,
> But to help us meet tomorrow . . .
> For growing trees are strengthened
> When they withstand the storm,
> And the sharp cut of the chisel
> Gives the marble grace and form.

"There was my answer," Dottie wrote to Helen. She wanted Helen to know how much the poem meant to her and also wanted to obtain copies she could mail to friends. Most of all, however, she wanted to let Helen know that her attitude toward life was beginning to change. "I read my copy a dozen times a day. I no longer think of what a burden I am and sit trying to figure out a way of ending it all . . . no doubt I'm here for a reason." Dottie, who at first was nervous about writing to Helen Steiner Rice even for copies of poems, never expected what came next.

A week after she wrote, Dottie received a lengthy, thoughtful reply from Helen. In that response and in subsequent letters, Helen did everything in her power to help Dottie look at adversity with a new and healing attitude. Helen first observed that Dottie should take heart from the fact that she had discovered a fundamental truth: Heartache is a universal experience. "I have read your letter many times," Helen began. "In those few pages many facets of life and our acceptance of what life brings us were revealed."

She then explained that the words of the poem that Dottie found so inspiring came, like all of her verses, from her own heart and her own experience. Specifically, she revealed that life had taught her to lean on God for encouragement and direction when nothing made sense. Dottie's life, according to Helen, was now teaching her the same lesson: "God tested you and he also tested your husband. You both went into the furnace of his love, and what a blest girl you are, for you came out of the flame with a newness of life and a beauty that can be gained only through this process."

Helen reassured Dottie that the answers to all of her questions were within reach. She wrote, "While you found the answer in my verse, the answer was really buried *inside of you by God,* but it just took something to make you recognize it." Helen concluded by encouraging Dottie to think of adversity as a force that could transform her. "You have gone through a great experience in living, and it has prepared you for a richer, fuller life wherever God decides to use you," she wrote.

Dottie was stunned that someone of Helen Steiner Rice's popularity and stature would take the time to counsel her. "How on earth do you ever thank someone, the *only* one who has made you see the light?" she wrote in response to Helen's letter. Unknown to her, the acknowledgment came in Dottie's transformation, which continued over a period of months. After studying the poem "When Trouble Comes and Things Go Wrong!" Dottie realized that she had unfairly blamed her friends for not being supportive when they were powerless to help her solve uniquely personal problems. When she read the lines of the poem and considered them, Dottie realized that what she had needed all along was faith in God.

> So do not tell your neighbor,
> your companion or your friend
> In the hope that they can help you
> bring your troubles to an end . . .
> For they, too, have their problems,
> they are burdened just like you,
> So take your cross to Jesus
> and He will see you through.

She sent the poem to her friends and asked their forgiveness. More compassionate now, she discovered a special affection for those who were as confined as she had been, so she began to distribute Helen's poems in local rest homes. And she passed out copies to her favorite merchants and her doctors. The response amazed her. "I had no idea so many people were troubled like *I was—before you*," she wrote to Helen.

Helen was immensely gratified by the change she observed in Dottie over the months following their first contact. "I can see from your letter that you are giving yourself away, and nothing enriches us so much as when we do that. For we become

71

so engrossed in doing for others that we completely forget about our own troubles." As the years passed, Dottie continued to send Christmas cards to Helen, and each one of them bore a message of thanks similar to this one: "You saved my life nine years ago with your beautiful writings and the letter that gave me back my faith. Thank you again, and again, and again."

Dottie's first response to adversity had been one of outrage at how God, her husband, and her friends had let her down. The way individuals react when adversity first strikes varies widely, as we see in the story of Eddie.

The Story of Eddie

Eddie was a young man who worked with Helen Steiner Rice at Gibson Greetings. When he had to leave his job because of illness, Helen gave comfort by urging him not to let fear of what might happen paralyze him. In a letter that delicately balanced compassion with sound advice, she outlined a program for triumphing over adversity that echoes her counsel to Dottie.

"Trouble comes to us all, and it is difficult sometimes to understand why suddenly a dark cloud appears on our horizon," Helen wrote, affirming that the fear and concern he felt were a natural result of this unforeseen crisis. But she then suggested that Eddie view his illness from a spiritual perspective rather than waste energy trying to grasp why he had been afflicted: "Our tomorrows are in eternal hands and they are safe there. There are no disappointments to those whose wills are stayed in the will of God." In concluding, Helen pressed her coworker to try to learn as much as possible from this misfortune. "I think with each troubled experience God gives us the opportunity to grow in soul stature," she counseled. Helen was keenly aware that she had no power to ease Eddie's physical pain, so she did what she could by reassuring him with her support and prayer:

> I don't know anything much that I can do that will help you very much. I can only commend you into God's care, and my prayer will be that God will grant you a calm, steadfast mind and patience to meet whatever comes with courage and faith.

Prayers, kind words, and reassurances were not just empty if well-meaning phrases when they came from Helen Steiner Rice. They invariably had substance and profoundly affected the recipient, as Melba, another of Helen's friends, discovered when she desperately needed help in contending with her fear.

The Story of Melba

Melba Heckman was the housekeeper of Helen's lifelong friends the Gradisons. She had long been an admirer of Helen Steiner Rice, loved her poetry, and read it faithfully. In January 1967 Melba suddenly found herself facing hospitalization and major surgery. Naturally she was fearful of the outcome and at a loss as to how she might bring her terror under control. During periods of intense pain and its accompanying mental anguish Melba relied heavily on her faith and especially on the poems Helen had sent her. "When things get to where I don't know how much more I can take, I sit down and read through everything you gave me and I get so much help and strength," she wrote to Helen shortly before her admission to the hospital.

Melba did, however, have a special request of Helen. It was one, she said, that meant more to her than anything she had ever asked of anyone. "Would you send me a little 'uplift poem,'

73

one that I could take with me to sort of bolster me up?" she wrote. Melba knew she would have Helen's prayers, but in her anxiety she believed that some special poem would make a vital difference both in her outlook and her recovery: "I'll look every day for word from you and if I receive it, I'll treasure it all my life."

Helen answered Melba's plea for help in a few days. She not only sent poems for Melba to take with her to the hospital, but she also enclosed the verses in a letter that outlined a plan of meditation designed to help restore Melba's peace of mind. She advocated that Melba read the Twenty-third Psalm very slowly and carefully each morning when she awakened and then read it again the same way after each meal and at bedtime. She continued:

> Just think what it means to know that THE LORD IS YOUR SHEPHERD and that HE IS LEADING YOU AND ANOINTING YOUR SCARS AND HEART-HURT WITH THE BALM OF HIS LOVE. The more you think about this the more you become aware of its power. You can heal your body and mind and heart with this Psalm.

Helen recommended that Melba continue this practice over a period of weeks. "You will be surprised how calm and wonderful you feel," she assured her.

Melba made it through her surgery and she eagerly reported to Helen how the letter and poems had buoyed her spirits. "There's nothing I can say that could begin to tell you how happy your lovely letter and beautiful poems made me." Throughout her convalescence Melba particularly relied on these words in "Daily Prayers Dissolve Your Cares":

> No day is unmeetable
> If on rising our first thought
> Is to thank God for the blessings
> That His loving care has brought.

Daily Prayers Dissolve Your Cares

I meet God in the morning
And go with Him through the day,
Then in the stillness of the night
Before sleep comes I pray
That God will just "take over"
All the problems I couldn't solve
And in the peacefulness of sleep
My cares will all dissolve,
So when I open up my eyes
To greet another day
I'll find myself renewed in strength
And there'll open up a way
To meet what seemed impossible
For me to solve alone
And once again I'll be assured
I am never "on my own" . . .
For if we try to stand alone
We are weak and we will fall,
For God is always *Greatest*
When we're helpless, lost and small,
And no day is unmeetable
If on rising our first thought
Is to thank God for the blessings
That His loving care has brought . . .
For there can be no failures
Or hopeless, unsaved sinners
If we enlist the help of God
Who makes all losers winners . . .
So meet Him in the morning
And go with Him through the day
And thank Him for His guidance
Each evening when you pray,
And if you follow faithfully
This daily way to pray
You will never in your lifetime
Face another "hopeless day."

Some time later Melba wrote to Helen, "I'll never be able to thank you enough. There was a time when I was about ready to give up." She said in closing that her own faith, the support of her minister, and the encouragement of Helen's words gave her the help and courage to pull through.

Often the letters Helen received from the brokenhearted reduced her to tears. "My son-in-law is still in a complete coma, and we are into our third year," wrote one distraught woman. Like Etta Hoeh, she had managed to find comfort in the poem "Let Not Your Heart Be Troubled." Later she expressed how grateful she was to Helen for composing the words that gave her family what she called "a little lift." "The 'End of the Road' poem has particular meaning to my daughter, my husband, and myself," she declared, "as many times we have felt that we were 'At the End of the Road' truly, but somehow God has given us the additional courage we have needed to carry on."

Helen found the countless facets of adversity intriguing, and she tried to explain her thoughts on the subject in numerous letters of advice and comfort. In 1974, for example, she corresponded with Bruce, a paraplegic.

The Story of Bruce

Bruce was a young man who was undergoing extensive therapy to regain the use of his legs. Helen advised him:

Paradoxical though it is, there is nothing in life worthwhile that is not attained through suffering and conflict. But suffering and sorrow are not too great a price to pay for the enriching privilege of touching other lives with more compassion and deeper understanding. All the sweetest things in life come to us on the "wings of pain and tears," giving us a new awareness of God's greatness, His goodness, and His grace!

76

And yet while she knew that in the end human suffering was an unfathomable, divine mystery, Helen also realized that it was important to encourage those who suffer to offer their adversity to God, who is able to transform it into spiritual lessons.

Helen wrote again to Bruce during the months of his recuperation, reminding him that he had already made great strides in his battle against adversity. "I know you are having a difficult struggle trying to master and manipulate your new walking gear," she wrote in a letter celebrating his birthday. "You have been so patient, so remarkable, tenacious and determined to rise above your limitations and hindrances, I want to urge you to never give up."

Helen also understood that Bruce would need to renew his courage on a daily basis. "Don't ever think, 'Oh, gee, what's the use,'" she reminded him. Helen prodded him to keep in mind the strength of character that had enabled him to persevere thus far and also to continue relying on God's help. "It takes PERSEVERANCE to just keep on going when the strong winds of doubt keep constantly blowing," she reminded him. Despite Bruce's frustration in the face of many disappointments, Helen insisted to him, "You are an inspiring example to so many people!"

Helen was convinced that those who faced adversity with a gallant attitude not only helped themselves, but also with equal impact touched the lives of those who witnessed their efforts. This definitely has proven true in the case of Dorothy Carey, whose battle against adversity has made her, in the words of her daughter-in-law, Tonya, "an inspiration to all who know her." Tonya says that Helen Steiner Rice's poem "Storms Bring Out the Eagles, but the Little Birds Take Cover" epitomizes Dorothy Carey's approach to every aspect of her life. Certainly adversity has prompted Dorothy to soar above the troubles that have befallen her in recent years.

Storms Bring Out the Eagles,
but the Little Birds Take Cover

When the "storms of life" gather darkly ahead,
I think of these wonderful words I once read
And I say to myself as "threatening clouds" hover
Don't "fold up your wings" and "run for cover"
But like the eagle "spread wide your wings,"
And "soar far above" the trouble life brings,
For the eagle knows that the higher he flies
The more tranquil and brighter become the skies
And there is nothing in life God ever asks us to bear
That we can't soar above "on the wings of prayer,"
And in looking back over the "storm you passed
   through"
You'll find you gained strength and new courage, too
For in facing "life's storms" with an eagle's wings
You can fly far above earth's small, petty things.

The Story of Dorothy

In January 1991 Dorothy's husband, Don, was transferred from Cincinnati, Ohio, to Idaho Falls, Idaho. She sold their home, and as she prepared to join him, word reached her that her mother-in-law in Texas had suffered what appeared to be a stroke. Dorothy went to Texas, gathered her mother-in-law's possessions, and moved the ailing woman with her to Idaho. She cared for her mother-in-law for three months until the elderly woman died.

Just as Dorothy thought her life might return to normal, she discovered a lump in her right breast. A biopsy showed it to be a fast-growing malignancy. "The hardest thing I have ever had to do was to call our children in Idaho, Illinois, and Virginia ten days before Christmas and tell them I had breast cancer," remembers Dorothy. She was quickly scheduled for a modified radical mastectomy.

Dorothy's initial response to the diagnosis was, not surprisingly, despair. "I felt I had been given a death sentence and I didn't even feel I could share this feeling with Don," she wrote. "I was exhausted and at the end of my rope. . . . I cried out to God, 'I can't do this.'" Then Dorothy remembered her mother had always told her, "God never gives you more than you can carry."

That advice mirrored the philosophy of Helen Steiner Rice, whose poem about the courage of the eagle includes these lines:

> And there is nothing in life God ever asks us to bear
> That we can't soar above "on the Wings of Prayer."

Helen's poems had always lifted Dorothy's spirits. Now she began to embody the attitude of the eagle. She used prayer to soar above her fear; through the minister at her new church she met a woman in the congregation who had survived the same surgery. Additional support came from old and new friends who had undergone mastectomies, and by the time Dorothy was admitted to the hospital she says she "was really at peace."

Dorothy's operation went well. The day after surgery she began simple exercises so she would not lose mobility in her shoulder. Before her release on Christmas Eve, however, she learned that she would have to undergo chemotherapy. During chemotherapy Dorothy lost all of her hair but not her sense of humor. "Being bald is not the worst thing that can happen to you—it is ONLY TEMPORARY," she comments; "to cancer patients, scars and bald heads become our badges of survival."

Dorothy finished her treatments in July 1992. The words of her favorite Helen Steiner Rice poem once again proved true. She indeed gained "strength and new courage" from the storm she had passed through. Tonya Carey marvels at her mother-in-law's great faith. "She is a loving wife, a wonderful role model for her children and grandchildren, and offers support, encouragement, and education about breast cancer to other women," writes Tonya. Dorothy Carey looks to the poetry of Helen Steiner Rice as one way God enables her to turn her own adversity into support for others. "I have most of her books," she says, "and I know I can always find a poem to suit the need of anyone I hear of with a special need."

Dorothy's story suggests that body and spirit may heal together as one overcomes adversity. But what about situations in which physical ills do not play a part? Helen's pattern for dealing with adversity by accepting our troubles, seeking God's help, and learning a lesson seems to work well in other circumstances also, as we see in the case of Paula.

The Story of Paula

Paula was in prison when friends sent her a book of verses that contained one poem that especially moved her, "Good Morning, God!" Paula was already familiar with Helen's writings but as she waited for the time of her release, this poem took on special meaning.

> Forgive the many errors
> That I made yesterday
> And let me try again, dear God,
> To walk closer in Thy way.

Those words had a profound effect on the prisoner. They did nothing less than change her life. For Paula the poems of Helen Steiner Rice became an unexpected blessing when she was despairing and most vulnerable. But they did not merely make her feel better; they gave her a chance to share her newly discovered hope for the future with the other women in the prison.

Paula's experience illustrates that Helen's pattern for healing the spirit works in many situations. Maria is also sustained by Helen's poems, but her story is quite different from Paula's, as is the experience of little Tara.

The Story of Maria

Maria relies on the poetry of Helen Steiner Rice to help her heal while she recovers from an abusive childhood. Helen's words have become what she calls "a trusted friend," one she can count on as she strives to mend both the emotional and physical scars of her early years. Now a woman in her thirties, Maria still finds it difficult to make peace with her past. "I still resent the damage that the wounds are costing me," she says. Nevertheless she loves Helen's poem "Flowers Leave Their Fragrance on the Hand That Bestows Them" because the verses remind her of all the friends who have touched her life and helped her heal. For Maria the poetry of Helen Steiner Rice is "a balm for the pain and confusion" she sees in her path. As she looks for God's guidance and attempts to follow Helen's advice, she tries to maintain a sense of humor: "Let me assure you that the Old Testament prophets had it easy. The Lord appeared to them in dreams and burning bushes; we can't claim that benefit." Maria's humor does not diminish the fact that Helen's poetry helped her through a time in her life when she needed to draw more deeply on her own faith. Maria admits as much when she writes, "Often it is your verses that attune me to the Lord faster than the Bible."

The Story of Tara

At the age of only ten, Tara has already learned to rely on the messages of Helen Steiner Rice to face adversity. Bad times are not reserved for adults. Tara loves Helen's poem "Each Day Brings a Chance to Do Better" because it is "just so real." Tara and her siblings were taken away from their mother and placed in foster care because their mom was ordered into a drug abuse recovery program. Tara knows her mother is trying "with all her might" to get her children back. Tara often reads her favorite Helen Steiner Rice poem, for its opening lines remind her of her mother:

> How often we wish for another chance
> To make a fresh beginning,
> A chance to blot out our mistakes
> And change failure into winning.

The section of the poem that encourages people to try with all their hearts "to live a little better" makes Tara think about

Each Day Brings a Chance to Do Better

How often we wish for another chance
To make a fresh beginning,
A chance to blot out our mistakes
And change failure into winning—
And it does not take a special time
To make a brand-new start,
It only takes the deep desire
To try with all our heart
To live a little better
And to always be forgiving
And to add a little "sunshine"
To the world in which we're living—
So never give up in despair
And think that you are through,
For there's always a tomorrow
And a chance to start anew.

her mother's hope to make her family one again. These words encourage Tara to believe that is going to happen someday.

"To make fine wine the grapes must be crushed and to make bread to feed the hungry people the wheat must be ground," Helen once wrote to a suffering friend. She believed we must be broken if we hope to grow according to God's higher plan. The ability to look at personal problems as symbolic opportunities for growth and not something God has sent as a punishment is the cornerstone of the healing process that Helen advocates.

Helen often told her friends, "God graduates the greatest scholars from the school of suffering." The inspiring stories in this chapter all bear poignant witness to the truth of that observation. Each of us faces formidable challenges we could never have anticipated. We can choose, as Etta, Dorothy, and the others did, to transform our own pain into lessons that change our lives. We can become wiser and kinder people who enrich the lives of others. If we follow the example of Helen Steiner Rice, we too will learn from experience the simple truth in the words "In God's hands adversity can make the heart rejoice."

Helen's Pattern for Healing the Pain of Adversity

1. Understanding that troubles are part of life.

Ask yourself: Can I accept the principle that adversity is part of the challenge of living? Have I reflected on the fact that many people all over the world are suffering from exactly the same kind of heartache as I am right at this moment?

2. Surrendering the outcome to God.

Ask yourself: Can I realize the futility of lapsing into self-pity and asking why me? Can I accept the fact that I may not be able to make things conform to my idea of the best possible outcome? Can I pray for guidance and surrender the result into God's hands?

3. Developing as a person through adversity.

Ask yourself: Can I turn my own pain into a lesson that will benefit me in the future? Through what I have learned from my heartache, can I increase my ability to help others? Can I bless my experience and see it as a teacher of wisdom?

Four

Healing the Pain of Loneliness

God's kindness is ever around you
Always ready to freely impart
Strength to your faltering spirit
Cheer to your lonely heart.

oneliness overtakes us when we feel separated from others. That isolation may be physical, for instance when someone lives alone without a support system of family or friends. It may also be more of an emotional phenomenon arising from a lost relationship, for example when a spouse dies, a marriage ends in divorce, or a dear friend moves away. Loneliness can be even more subtle and not associated with the issue of physical separation at all. Teenagers often suffer profound loneliness in the midst of great activity, particularly when they feel rejected by their peers. Adults experience it too when they feel a deep, painful alienation from others despite successful careers, financial security, and social acceptance.

Everybody Needs Someone

Everybody, everywhere,
No matter what their station,
Has moments of deep loneliness
And quiet desperation,
For this lost and lonely feeling
Is inherent in mankind—
It is just the Spirit speaking
As God tries again to find
An opening in the "worldly wall"
We build against God's touch,
For we feel so self-sufficient
That we do not need God much,
So we vainly go on struggling
To find some explanation
For these disturbing, lonely moods
Of inner isolation . . .
But the answer keeps eluding us
For in our selfish, finite minds
We do not even recognize
That we cannot ever find
The reason for life's emptiness
Unless we learn to share
The problems and the burdens
That surround us everywhere—
But when our eyes are opened
And we look with love at others
We begin to see not strangers
But our sisters and our brothers . . .
So open up your hardened hearts
And let God enter in—
He only wants to help you
A new life to begin . . .
And every day's a good day
To lose yourself in others
And any time a good time
To see mankind as brothers,
And this can only happen
When you realize it's true
That everyone needs someone
And that someone is you!

No matter what its source or form, the agony of loneliness desperately seeks relief. Some choose to deaden it by distracting or anesthetizing themselves, using television, food, alcohol, or drugs to escape the anguish. Others keep it at bay by working themselves to distraction or overbooking their social schedules. None of these efforts ultimately prove to be successful, for they address the symptom, not the disease. Helen Steiner Rice suggested a positive way in which to deal with loneliness. She believed that despite its devastating effect, loneliness is a state of mind that offers us a choice: We can either surrender to it or transcend it. If we focus on our ability to make connections with others and with God, Helen advised, rather than on our feelings of isolation, we soon realize that we are never alone.

Helen did not develop her ability to overcome loneliness by dispassionately observing the heartache of friends and correspondents. She knew its pain all too well from personal experience. She freely admitted that she was regularly drawn into periods of what she characterized as "lost-loneliness," times when she felt misunderstood, alienated, and lonely. That she often suffered through these episodes is hardly surprising, since she lived alone in a hotel room for almost half a century. Moreover, during the eight decades of her life the world changed so dramatically and at such breakneck speed that she often felt profoundly estranged and completely out of touch, even with her contemporaries.

Helen expressed her intimate knowledge of the agonizing forms that loneliness can take in poems and letters. It is part of the universal experience of living, she explained. She expressed this idea in her poem "Everybody Needs Someone."

> Everybody, everywhere,
> No matter what their station,
> Has moments of deep loneliness
> And quiet desperation.

Sooner or later we all feel separated from others, even our closest friends and relatives, in some way. When that happens and we feel painfully alone, it inevitably brings us to a moment of truth. This is a critical time in our lives—one when we must pause, reflect, and come to recognize that loneliness is in fact an invitation. It is a call to understand the nature of our spiritual connection to God and our relationship to others. Helen promised that if we can look at our loneliness as symbolic—as more than just the feeling of misery—we will discover something quite extraordinary: We only feel lonely when we have no other focus than ourselves.

In her writing, Helen emphasized that the best way to heal loneliness is by shifting the point of concentration away from ourselves. Try connecting to someone else in a sincere and meaningful way, she urged; you will be surprised at how much better it makes you feel! Helen practiced this approach in her own life. She supported her friends with daily acts of kindness and she spread her message far and wide through her correspondence with hundreds of lonely people who responded to her poems. The most important connection for Helen in wrestling with loneliness, however, was conversation with God in prayer. As she put it, if you talk to God, then you can believe that "Someone is listening, and if Someone is there listening, you are never really alone." This chapter begins with the story of Pamela, who matured through her loneliness with the help of the poetry of Helen Steiner Rice.

The Story of Pamela

Teenagers fight the war against isolation on many fronts. They bounce between emotional highs and lows and constantly wage battles for independence, but at the same time they experience a deep dependence that emanates from a need to feel accepted by their peers. Thirteen-year-old Pamela Headley faced a particularly difficult situation. The girls at her school alternately ignored her and teased her mercilessly. One Friday night after an especially difficult day at school Pamela came home and told her parents that she could not cope with the situation any longer. Frustrated beyond measure, she vowed never to return to a school where she was continually rejected by other students.

Pamela's parents listened sympathetically and then told her that she could count on their support if she chose to change schools. They pointed out, however, that she would be finishing her classes at that school in only two months, so there were certain disadvantages in transferring. After the exchange of views Pamela and her parents prayed as a family. Once she had taken everything into account, she decided she would stay at her school and try to finish out the school year.

Realizing how upset her daughter was, Pamela's mother gave her a slip of paper on which she had written Helen's poem "This Too Will Pass Away" before she went to bed that night. It opens with these lines:

> If I can endure for this minute
> Whatever is happening to me
> No matter how heavy my heart is
> Or how "dark" the moment may be . . .

When Pamela read the poem, she began to cry. It not only described her feelings exactly, but it also suggested an answer to her questions and offered a promise of hope. If she could remain secure in the knowledge God loved her, then she would not be defeated by what seemed like an intolerable set of circumstances.

> Then nothing in life can defeat me
> For as long as this knowledge remains
> I can suffer whatever is happening
> For I know God will break "all the chains" . . .

91

This Too Will Pass Away

If I can endure for this minute
Whatever is happening to me
No matter how heavy my heart is
Or how "dark" the moment may be—
If I can remain calm and quiet
With all my world crashing about me
Secure in the knowledge God loves me
When everyone else seems to doubt me—
If I can but keep on believing
What I know in my heart to be true,
That "darkness will fade with the morning"
And that this will pass away, too—
Then nothing in life can defeat me
For as long as this knowledge remains
I can suffer whatever is happening
For I know God will break "all the chains"
That are binding me tight in "the darkness"
And trying to fill me with fear—
For there is no night without dawning
And I know that "my morning" is near.

The poem brought about a transformation in Pamela and she wrote:

> I can't express in words the relief and hope that I felt after I read that poem. I read it again and again until I was practically sobbing with relief. I realized once again that God was in control, and that if I just trusted in him, then "this too shall pass."

Because of the revelation Helen's poem had sparked, Pamela realized that she had come to rely more and more on God as she struggled through those three miserable years at her middle school. "I just needed a little reminder that I needed to stop feeling sorry for myself, and start trusting God. . . . I believe God led my mother's hands to that piece of paper that day," she says.

Pamela learned a lot from her experience of loneliness. Like Helen Steiner Rice, she grew in an awareness of God's continuous presence with her. She now places even the unhappy events of her life in a spiritual perspective.

> We are going to go through times in our life when we feel like we just can't go on. . . . It is times like this when God gives us encouragement in the form of a person, Bible verse, or poem. He gives us the message that if we can just keep on keeping on, then whatever the struggles we are facing will pass away. This is what Mrs. Rice's poem told me. It gave me the courage and strength to go on with God's help.

Pamela Headley succeeded admirably in putting into practice Helen's prescription for healing loneliness. Helen knew, however, that loneliness is not the kind of problem one can solve once and for all. In the course of daily living many things can cause loneliness to return again and again, and every time it does we must make a choice in how we deal with it. For her part Helen, try as she might to fend it off, found that loneliness often swept over her, especially when she thought of her husband. In an October 1970 letter to her friend Mary Jane, Helen described the way it sometimes overcame her:

> I have experienced this feeling of "lost-loneliness" many times through the thirty-eight years that Franklin has been gone, and it seems a mist of melancholia drifts in like a fog and there is nothing I can do until the fog lifts. But I know that THIS, TOO, WILL PASS AWAY.

Helen's experience influenced her counsel to a lonely woman named Karen.

The Story of Karen

Helen believed that even though she could not escape the pain of loneliness, the least she could do was meet it head-on. Her usual response was to acknowledge her feelings honestly, then shift her attention away from herself. This was the same method she recommended to Karen, a troubled young coworker. She started by affirming Karen's feelings. "Honey, no one ever went through life without getting lost in the labyrinth of loneliness or falling into a dungeon of darkness," she wrote. But Helen also knew that a change of outlook could prevent Karen from becoming a victim of prolonged loneliness. She explained to the young woman, "Unexpectedly and very gently the misty fog is going to be lifted from your mind." Helen prompted Karen to shift her attention beyond her own feelings of sadness toward her connections with others at her job, saying, "Dear, we need you and you need us!" Realizing that a part of loneliness can spring from feelings of worthlessness, Helen then elaborated on Karen's value to others: "Keep remembering you have so much to give this world! You have beauty, sensitivity, beautiful eyes that can see and beautiful hands that can feel, and you are here on this earth to INSPIRE OTHER PEOPLE!"

Helen knew from experience that a sure way to lift herself out of loneliness was to make an effort to touch the life of another in kindness, to make a connection that helped counteract the feelings of separation. She also believed, however, that feelings of loneliness were more than a sense of isolation; they spoke of a deeper need. To Helen they symbolized a fundamental yearning in the soul, a desire within the depths of each human being not just to relate to other people, but also to feel the divine connection of being one with God. The emptiness this longing awakened was a spiritual one that Helen knew could never be satisfied by anything less than a genuine relationship with God. "I realize," she wrote to her friend Dora in 1974, "all that this world has to give me is fleeting, and to try to fill up the empty places in my life with material things leaves me more empty than before." Since the hunger that was the main symptom of loneliness was in the end a hunger for God, only God could fill it. It was the comfort of God's presence that Helen's poetry powerfully conveyed to Nelle, who overcame her loneliness and isolation by offering joy to others despite being housebound in a small third-floor apartment.

The Story of Nelle

"Your beautiful letter . . . made me feel like a three-year-old who had received a first dollar which she could really call her very own," a thrilled Nelle Methe wrote to Helen Steiner Rice in the spring of 1965. With good reason Nelle treasured every connection to the world outside her small home. Unable to walk without the aid of crutches, the seventy-eight-year-old woman was confined in an apartment that was only accessible by stairs too steep for her to negotiate.

Nelle's enforced isolation was especially difficult because she had such an outgoing personality. For

forty years she had traveled all over the country for Sears, Roe-
buck and Company, serving as she characterized it as a "system
installer, trouble shooter, and peacemaker." Not long after her
retirement the elderly businesswoman's legs began to fail her
and soon she found herself entirely dependent on a pair of
crutches. Six weeks at a rehabilitation center helped control the
terrible spasms in Nelle's legs, but her doctors said that was only
the first step toward recovery. She needed an additional eight to
ten months of therapy to regain sufficient strength in her mus-
cles to walk unaided. The cost as well as the length of stay made
it impossible for her to move on to the next stage of treatment.
As a result Nelle could neither leave her apartment nor under-
take the medical treatment that might make her ambulatory again.
She refused, however, to let her misfortune get the upper hand.

Long familiar with the greeting cards signed by Helen Steiner
Rice, Nelle had always found Helen's verses both comforting
and uplifting. Since she could no longer leave her home to
buy cards or booklets, Nelle was concerned about how she
would continue reading Helen's inspiring words. In April 1965
the solution to the problem came to her; she simply wrote to
Helen in Cincinnati. "I have hungered for your poems for sev-
eral years," she explained, adding, "Your writing is full of the
love and understanding that is so much needed in our lives
today." She concluded the letter by asking Helen for copies of
booklets and poems and enclosed a check to cover the cost.
In return Nelle received a large envelope containing Helen's
letter of response and a packet of poems for Nelle's personal
use. She was overwhelmed, acknowledging that Helen's
thoughtfulness had produced "the most wonderful experience
I've had in many years."

Nelle's letter had revealed that the elderly woman possessed
an energetic and faith-filled spirit. "You are a very remarkable
lady," Helen observed; "your handwriting is distinctive and
firm and your mind keen and responsive, so God has indeed
blessed your seventy-eight years." Those words of support

prompted Nelle to take action. She decided that even while confined to her apartment, there were many things she could still do. First, she called the Chicago office of Gibson Greetings and discovered which stores stocked Helen's cards. Then she made special arrangements to have cards and booklets mailed to her in quantity. When she was told that some items were in short supply, she had her favorite verses mimeographed. Once everything was in place, Nelle went to work. She began to reach out to others far and wide, using Helen's poems to let people know that someone actually cared about them.

A widow who suffered from a birth defect that prevented her from bearing children, Nelle filled the emptiness in her life by corresponding with pen pals around the world. Some were young soldiers then serving in Vietnam. Along with newsy letters, she sent them mimeographed copies of Helen Steiner Rice's poems and even prevailed on Helen to autograph a dozen copies of her booklet "For Those in the Service of Their Country." Nelle also loved the poem "When Trouble Comes and Things Go Wrong" and she enthusiastically informed Helen, "I have a list already for at least fifty names who will surely receive it as soon as I have these mimeoed."

However, Nelle did not confine her use of Helen's verses to creating a loving connection between herself and others around the country and overseas; she also relied on favorite poems to renew her own connection with God. Helen's words reminded Nelle so clearly of God's constant nearness to her that at one point she praised Helen for telling "the story of our God . . . in such understandable English." Thanks to Helen, the housebound woman felt her relationship with God flourish. "Never in my life have I felt so close to our dear God," she wrote to Helen. She attributed her newly discovered joy as much to Helen's verses as she did to Helen's obviously sincere interest in her well-being. "Oh my dear Honey," she explained, "I feel so rich and different since I have known you."

Eventually Nelle created a three-way connection among Helen, herself, and God by using the verses of "My Daily Prayer," which she felt captured "such a real honest-to-God understanding of human nature." She promised Helen she would recite the words every morning at seven o'clock just as Helen did. "Then, dear friend, we will be thinking of our heavenly Father and each other!" Helen helped Nelle realize that there was no time for self-pitying loneliness, that life was filled with moments she could use to comfort others and opportunities to cherish the presence of God in everyday life.

Nelle learned what Helen already recognized—that conquering loneliness required breaking out of one's isolation enough to touch the life of another. Lila, one of Helen's friends who suffered from the misery of alcoholism, recognized the wisdom of Helen's systematic approach to defeating loneliness after she received one of Helen's Christmas cards.

The Story of Lila

Lila had tried to numb the pain of her loneliness by drinking. At first, she enjoyed the temporary euphoria that liquor brought, mostly because it took her mind off feelings of isolation. Soon, however, she became an alcoholic, dependent on gradually increasing doses of liquor to briefly improve her spirits. Finally, her addiction drove her to what she described as a "tragic state," which nearly cost her marriage and the custody of her child. She struggled without success to battle the disease on her own. Her family doctor and a psychiatrist did their best to help but eventually gave up on her, which only served to drive her deeper into despair. In a last desperate attempt to save herself she went to another physician, who suggested that Lila try Alcoholics Anonymous.

My Daily Prayer

Bless me, heavenly Father,
Forgive my erring ways,
Grant me strength to serve Thee,
Put purpose in my days.
Give me understanding
Enough to make me kind
So I may judge all people
With my heart and not my mind.
And teach me to be patient
In everything I do,
Content to trust Your wisdom
And to follow after You.
And help me when I falter
And hear me when I pray
And receive me in Thy kingdom
To dwell with Thee some day.

Lila joined AA and after she had been in the program for almost three years, she wrote to Helen, "I am happy and grateful to be able to say that I have not had a drink since." Alcoholics Anonymous, Lila explained, followed a twelve-step program for recovery that concentrated on the spiritual aspects of the ailment. Its purpose was engendering a complete change of attitude, and as part of the twelfth step, the plan encouraged recovering alcoholics to carry their message of healing to others. This aspect of the program seemed to mean the most to Lila, for in explaining it to Helen she wrote, "It is in trying to help others in trouble that we maintain our sobriety." As part of her recovery Lila had become a regular speaker in the AA program. Her work gave her ties with others that helped fill the painful emptiness that had first led her into drinking.

When she received Helen's Christmas card, Lila was elated, for she immediately saw how helpful it would be in her lecture work. She explained in a letter to Helen how effectively the words of her card could be translated into the support group's message to other alcoholics:

> Nothing I write the whole year through
> Means more to me than this card to you
> For you're more to me than a name and a face . . .

Letting other alcoholics know that she wanted so desperately to help and that they were more than just "a name and face" was paramount to Lila.

The next lines of Helen's card also captured Lila's feelings perfectly:

> For only through folks I have met like you
> Can the promise of Christmas ever come true.

Only through sharing what she had gained, Lila wrote to Helen, and carrying her message to other alcoholics could she hope to maintain her own peace of mind.

The poem's words of Christmas greeting and affirmation continued in a language she understood:

> To send Christmas greetings is only the start
> Of something deeper that's hidden inside
> That we cover up with an "armor of pride"
> But from time to time, it's bound to peek through
> And I've glimpsed it often in folks like you.

Taking her message to other alcoholics was Lila's first step toward releasing them from the "terrible trap" they were in. She also wanted to reveal their potential. Indeed, the simple act of sharing the details of their mutual problems contributed immeasurably to healing. Lila wrote, "Never have I known the understanding that is brought about through common suffering."

Studying Helen's poem, Lila realized that it articulated her thought on a higher level:

> Somehow I feel you and I are a part
> Not just of each other but Christ's own heart
> And He came at Christmas so we might find
> That it's not enough to be casually kind
> For life can only be peaceful and good
> When we are loved and understood.

The twelve-step recovery program requires surrendering one's life and will to a Higher Power and making amends to those who have been harmed by one's addictive behavior. But there is something beyond that act of capitulation, Lila explained, because people in Alcoholics Anonymous were taught that being "casually kind" was not enough to complete the healing process. "You have to give of yourself in order to help the other guy," was the way she put it, and letting those she befriended know they were loved and understood was exactly what people in AA are reaching for, she said.

101

These lines summarized Lila's beliefs about recovery:

So blessed be the Christmas tie that binds
The love in our hearts to the thoughts in our minds . . .

To transform thoughts was at the heart and soul of the AA process. "Those thoughts . . . are what got us into trouble in the first place," she wrote. "They must be changed to eliminate self-pity, selfishness, resentments." How persuasively the verses of Helen's innocent and sincere Christmas card summarized the AA healing process!

The card had such a dramatic effect on Lila that she used it to close all of her talks at AA meetings, and she reported to Helen with the greatest sincerity how valuable it was: "I wish you could see the looks on the faces of men and women with a background of years of drinking—some out of mental institutions, some having been in jail." Lila thanked Helen for composing the verses on a Christmas card that meant so much to her and had reached so many others in Alcoholics Anonymous. "I don't suppose when you wrote this card that you ever dreamed that it would be used to encourage, inspire, and help a bunch of ex-drunks who represent a cross-section of life from top drawer to skid row. But I thought you might like to know."

Something deep inside her led Lila to recognize that the lonely person's connection with others and with God, so crucial to the twelve-step program of AA, was also the part of Helen's message for healing loneliness that mattered the most. But the pain of being alone, as Helen knew very well, manifested itself in many ways. Over the years Helen saw them all. Some who contacted her about feeling alone were not troubled by addictive behavior as Lila was. They were resentful because life in general seemed unfair and those around them appeared to be responsible for their unhappiness. They believed that they shouldn't have to deal with disquieting, unhappy, and lonely experiences—that somehow everything *should* just be different. In the fall of 1974 Helen encountered this way of looking at the world twice in one week, first from a disheartened woman whom Helen called her "lonely little Bluebird."

The Story of Bluebird

Bluebird was a woman who wrote to Helen expressing her despair. Gently Helen attempted to guide her onto a constructive course:

> I know so well how lonely and forsaken and helpless you feel, and I wish you could be transported into surroundings that would make you a happy little Bluebird again. But, in life, we cannot always change our surroundings. So the only thing we can do is change our attitude.

Helen believed that part of "Bluebird's" confusion arose from messages she heard from the world around her. The most destructive message of all, Helen thought, was the foolish notion that people should not have to wrestle with uncomfortable feelings. To think so was simply to be willfully wrongheaded, Helen explained.

> While in our modern society we are led to believe that we can in some way free ourselves completely from these feelings, finally, if we practice the RIGHT METHODS, it really is not true. Life consists of carrying our cross and if we learn to do this regardless of the circumstances that surround us, we can turn our cross into a crown.

As chance would have it, Helen told Bluebird, she had just received a letter from another young woman, Nancy, who described similar feelings of loneliness and a "constant gnawing turmoil" inside of her that seemed to be tearing her apart. Feelings such as those experienced by these young women are not unique; they are an integral part of everyone's life, Helen tried to explain when she wrote, "I have come face to face with them many times in my long life." Nancy, after reading one of Helen's books of verses, had written to her asking for help. Helen did her best to oblige.

The Story of Nancy

Nancy was a twenty-one-year-old medical secretary who had few close friends. An only child whose parents were overly protective, she longed to go on dates but never did because she felt inept at making conversation and feared that young men would reject her. Furthermore, she felt undervalued in her job and believed that her potential was unrecognized and untapped. "I feel lost, confused, lonely, and life has no meaning for me," she lamented to Helen.

Nancy was honest and introspective enough to acknowledge that she really was unhappy with herself. "It feels as if someone is eating out the insides of my body, gnawing away until nothing will be left." To her credit, Nancy realized that she was filling that awful feeling of emptiness with jealousy:

I'm a shy, quiet person, therefore I'm jealous of those who are talkative and outgoing. . . . I'm jealous of those who are pretty and skinny because I'm not. I'm jealous of those who are happy because I'm not. The list can go on forever. Mrs. Rice, where does it all stop?

Within that plea for help Helen could see too little self-esteem and too much self-pity. She assured Nancy that she was not alone in experiencing feelings of anger, helplessness, and desolation:

Now, all those inner feelings that you are experiencing (and you describe so expertly) are not strangers to any of us. . . . I have often tangled with them on life's highway to heaven. So, do not concentrate on them, and most of all, remember that NO ONE CAN GO THROUGH LIFE WITHOUT EXPERIENCING THESE FEELINGS.

Helen tackled Nancy's poor self-image as well as she could, urging the young woman, "Thank God every day that you have such a keen, sensitive, and perceptive mind that makes it possible for you to entertain the thoughts that you expressed to me." Then she suggested that Nancy realize how much and in what manner she herself was contributing to her own unhappiness: "God has made you a beautiful, warm, wonderful person and He gave you spiritual consciousness which you have been using incorrectly by downgrading yourself instead of multiplying all your wonderful assets that you seem to be overlooking."

As one of God's children, Nancy was beautiful inside, Helen reassured her, saying, "If you only give it a chance, this spiritual beauty will shine through and it will draw other people to you like a magnet!"

Once Helen had laid the foundation for eliminating Nancy's self-pity and poor self-image, she went on to explain to the troubled woman what she needed to do next to escape from the prison of her loneliness: "Don't dwell on your shortcomings, dear. FOCUS ALL YOUR ATTENTION ON OTHERS, and you will find, in giving your love and attention to others, YOU, TOO, WILL BE ENRICHED."

The most practical, if not the easiest, way for Nancy to apply this advice was at the office where she spent most of the day. Helen sent her the verse "Brighten the Corner Where You Are" and advised, "That's just what I want you to do." She gave her a specific example:

You'll just never, never know the many times someone will walk in to see one of those doctors feeling fear, uncertainty, and anxi-

Brighten the Corner Where You Are

We cannot all be famous
Or be listed in "Who's Who,"
But every person great or small
Has important work to do,
For seldom do we realize
The importance of small deeds
Or to what degree of greatness
Unnoticed kindness leads—
For it's not the big celebrity
In a world of fame and praise
But it's doing unpretentiously
In undistinguished ways
The work that God assigned to us
Unimportant as it seems
That makes our task outstanding
And brings reality to dreams—
So do not sit and idly wish
For wider, new dimensions
Where you can put in practice
Your many "Good Intentions"—
But at the spot God placed you
Begin at once to do
Little things to brighten up
The lives surrounding you,
For if everybody brightened up
The spot on which they're standing
By being more considerate
And a little less demanding,
This dark old world would very soon
Eclipse the "Evening Star"
If everybody brightened up
The corner where they are!

ety, and one word of assurance from you or a certain smile on your face will transform you into a BEAUTIFUL, UNDERSTANDING LADY.

Nancy had a unique opportunity, Helen assured her, to be an "angel" to the people who crossed her path every day.

Nancy had written that somehow she already knew that only God could help her find her way but that she was afraid just to go and sit in church. Helen, using poetry and practical wisdom, gave Nancy a pathway out of her loneliness that began with an honest assessment of herself and ended in compassionate behavior toward others.

Sometimes practical answers to healing loneliness are far more elusive than they were for Nancy. For some, loneliness is born of a deep sense of alienation from what is occurring in the world around them. Helen was just as familiar with this face of loneliness as she was with its others. She once described to her friend Alberta how she felt on returning to her office after a period of illness: "Everything is strange and I feel disoriented, like a babe in the woods, struggling to find my way back into the swift pace of this busy, wicked world." The peculiar loneliness of being a stranger in one's own environment was precisely the heartache that plagued a Japanese woman who wrote to let Helen know how much comfort she derived from her faith and from Helen's poems.

The Story of Tamae

Tamae received a Helen Steiner Rice calendar and a book of poems as a gift from an American friend. Deeply moved by the sentiments expressed in the poems, Tamae contacted Helen in 1967 to let her know how profoundly they had affected her. The "poems and words are very fine," wrote Tamae. "Some are fit to my lonely heart." Tamae lived a solitary life on the outskirts of Tokyo. After her beloved companion, a dog named Mimi,

107

died during a severe heat wave when the household well dried up, Tamae was left utterly alone. Because she had been educated at an Episcopal mission school and converted to Christianity, she felt even more isolated in a culture where her religion was little understood. Indeed, only one of her teachers still lived nearby. Nevertheless Tamae devoutly practiced her Christian faith and found relief from her loneliness through her connection with a tiny Bible study class. To make matters worse, Tamae also suffered from a serious liver disorder but reported to Helen that she had entrusted her fate to God, adding, "By the will of God I shall soon become healthy." Despite living under such difficult conditions, Tamae proved to be a woman of remarkable faith.

Helen wrote Tamae a special poem, telling her, "Across thousands of miles and many seas you think of me and our hearts reach out to embrace each other."

> I think of you so many times
> And wish with all my heart
> That I could reach across the miles
> That keep us far apart . . .
> And somehow just COMMUNICATE
> The things I'd like to say
> If I were standing close to you
> Instead of FAR AWAY.

Helen's heartfelt effort to make a connection meant a great deal to Tamae. So too did Helen's reassurance that not only did she have the poet's friendship, but also she could always be sure of the presence of God in her life. "You and I know that our lives are in God's keeping and that we never walk alone. . . . May the good Lord keep His mighty hand on you and when the days are darkest may the light of His love come shining through," Helen told her.

Tamae promised to stay in contact with Helen by praying for her daily and she let Helen know that her lonely heart was filled with spiritual power from reading Helen's poems. "The beautiful poems that God sent me through you! It is like the treasure of spirit," she wrote.

As Helen got older she felt an ever deeper commitment to reach out to lonely people like Tamae. As her friends and colleagues of long standing began to die, she too experienced loneliness. She mused in a letter to her confidant Mary Jane, "One by one all my contemporaries seem to be leaving me standing alone on the 'sands of time.'" This perception reinforced Helen's determination to make as potent a connection as possible with anyone who reached out to her. She realized that many who wrote to her were part of "a vast, ever-increasing army of lonely people who are entrapped in the web time spins . . . leaving us empty-handed and alone." Helen indicated in a letter to another close friend, "My only aim in life is to reach the lost, lonely, . . . sick and sorrowing people. And just as long as I have one breath of life in me and one hand that can write, I intend to do this!" She never found herself wanting for opportunities.

Ellen was a soldier in that "army of lonely people." One of Helen's most faithful correspondents, she lived alone in an urban housing project.

The Story of Ellen

Until she wrote to Helen Steiner Rice in 1968, empty hours filled Ellen's lonely days. Then as if by magic her whole world changed when Helen replied to the letter she had written. Ellen suddenly had something to do, for she realized that many of those lonely hours could be filled conversing with Helen by mail. She began with enthusiasm to type letters of five, six, or even ten pages, all single-spaced, at one sitting. It was not unusual for her to write several of these lengthy missives to Helen each week, which was all the more amazing because she suffered from painful ulcers and blisters on her hands and between her fingers. Helen found the magnitude of this correspondence overwhelming but she understood that behind the letters was a woman with a sincere heart and a desperately lonely life.

Ellen's loneliness derived from her feeling that no one truly knew her. She had casual visitors now and then, certainly, and she treated each one with courtesy. On one day for instance an eighty-year-old retired schoolteacher dropped by to play geography games with her, and neighborhood children stopped and offered to run errands. Ellen chatted with the aged teacher; she gave one child a dime to mail a letter and another a dime to sweep the floor. Another time a new lady in the housing project visited because she too was lonely and had seen Ellen's warm smile from a distance. Ellen was not really all alone, but there was still something very important missing—the feeling that she was truly and deeply understood.

Her connection with Helen Steiner Rice transformed Ellen. Helen's letters made her feel as though she was truly appreciated. Once, when Helen called her a co-heir to God's kingdom, Ellen responded by asking if she could really be as valuable to God as Helen Steiner Rice. Helen assured her that there was no doubt about it. Ellen then began pouring out stories of her life's heartaches, accounts of experiences she had locked inside herself for decades. Caring and sympathetic, Helen never judged her, so it is no surprise that she felt Helen understood everything. When she learned that Helen had been widowed at a young age, Ellen was firmly convinced that her new friend genuinely appreciated her loneliness.

Ellen's love of the Bible prompted her to reflect deeply and at length on the experience of loneliness, for she realized that

Jesus was often physically alone. "Alone in the desert for forty days," she enumerated for Helen, "alone at his trial before Pilate and before Herod. . . . He arose alone. He walked the road to Emmaus alone." But she believed that Jesus was never without the presence of his Father, even as she came to believe that she was never without the loving presence of God. "So we are never alone," she concluded to Helen. "I could be a most miserable creature if I wanted to trade on my loneliness." Because of Helen Steiner Rice, Ellen was able to choose a more wholesome and fulfilling path.

Helen did not have the time to answer all of Ellen's letters but she did promise that she would try to read every one. She told Ellen that she could feel free to use her as a "sounding board." "In telling me all these amazing stories and recounting your past life, you are by indirection contributing to the enlargement of my life," she wrote. Ellen's life took on an entirely new meaning because she felt that Helen valued her. To Ellen, Helen Steiner Rice's friendship was a clear demonstration of the extension of God's love.

Virginia's situation was quite different from Ellen's, but after her husband died, she too found relief from her loneliness through Helen's poems.

The Story of Virginia

Virginia's husband died suddenly, leaving her with a nineteen-year-old son who was mentally and physically handicapped beyond treatment and a healthy fifteen-year-old daughter. While she struggled to adjust to the loss of her spouse, Virginia decided that above all else she would not let bitterness and self-pity take control of her family's fate. Although things were, from her point of view, about as bad as they could be, she was certain that an answer would come through Helen Steiner Rice's poems, for they had always "reached the very depths" of her heart. Finding nowhere else to turn, she wrote to Helen, explaining that she believed "only one who had suffered deeply or had a very close contact with God would be able to put into words the messages" that Helen did.

Even though she felt terribly lonely, Virginia was familiar enough with Helen's counsel to know that the first step in healing her loneliness came in recognizing its power and facing it directly. Consequently she also understood that the next vital step in the healing process depended on comforting others. Armed with that knowledge, she asked Helen if she would help her find her way with "God's help to be a productive person who can be an inspiration to someone else."

Moved by Virginia's plea, Helen sent her a sympathetic letter, several poems, and other inspirational material that she believed would help her through this period of loneliness. Helen was not disappointed, for the healing soon began, as Virginia explained when she wrote to thank Helen:

> If, what you say in "How Great the Yield from a Fertile Field" is true, I shall rejoice in my broken heart and hope that God will feel that I am worthy to bring forth a rich harvest through me. . . . With God's help and your inspiration, may I also be an instrument of hope for someone I meet, who will also in turn pass it on to someone they meet—surely, there are many ways to be a disciple of God to help spread peace and understanding.

To Virginia, Helen's poetry offered a form of companionship on her road toward healing. In a different way it accompanies Ann on her journey through loneliness. At the age of ninety Ann is limited in what she can do, but she still lives on her own and takes pride in her independence.

112

The Story of Ann

Ann Walters relies heavily on the poetry of Helen Steiner Rice as a constant companion, particularly since the deaths of her brothers and sister over the last few years. The poem "The Joy of Unselfish Giving" encourages Ann to look beyond herself and empathize with others, despite the misery of collapsed vertebrae in her back that necessitate walking with a cane. The poem "God Is Never Beyond Our Reach" reminds her that she has more to be grateful for than she can measure and that she should never feel alone. Helen's poems help Ann maintain a positive attitude. "Every one is so inspiring and full of hope," writes Ann. She believes that God gave Helen "a special blessing to compose such beautiful and meaningful poems." Ann thanks God every day that she can still take care of herself. "Nieces and nephews live close by and are so good to me. I do a lot of praying every day and my life is all in God's Hands."

Although loneliness can be a terrifying state of being, Helen Steiner Rice believed its power could be harnessed by changing the direction of its force. If we look at it not as a deadly enemy, but rather as a divine call to form a closer union with others and a deeper reliance on God, then the whole character of the affliction changes. Helen advocated this approach in her poems and in the letters she sent to loyal correspondents she never met, like Nelle, Nancy, and Tamae. She stated it clearly in 1975, when she wrote to her good friend Ev, "I may feel a little lonely at times, but I am NEVER ALONE. I know my loneliness is just the soul trying to get back to the place it came from, and GOD IS NEVER MORE THAN A PRAYER AWAY."

While the first presentation of loneliness makes us acutely aware of ourselves and our pain, Helen believed its purpose was

113

God Is Never Beyond Our Reach

No one ever sought the Father
And found He was not there,
And no burden is too heavy
To be lightened by a prayer,
No problem is too intricate
And no sorrow that we face
Is too deep and devastating
To be softened by His grace,
No trials and tribulations
Are beyond what we can bear
If we share them with our Father
As we talk to Him in prayer—
And men of every color,
Every race and every creed
Have but to seek the Father
In their deepest hour of need—
God asks for no credentials,
He accepts us with our flaws,
He is kind and understanding
And He welcomes us because
We are His erring children
And He loves us every one,
And He freely and completely
Forgives all that we have done,
Asking only if we're ready
To follow where He leads—
Content that in His wisdom
He will answer all our needs.

to call us forth, to give us an invitation to cast off the chains of egotism and self-pity. She was quite sure that the great emptiness that was at the heart of being lonely could never be filled by earthly comforts: No amount of food, drink, possessions, or entertainment could satisfy it. Above all, she knew that overcoming loneliness requires faith. "Only GOD can really fill the GREAT VOID of our lives," Helen wrote to her friend Audrey. God does that, she believed, by relating to each of us personally through our human interactions and also through prayer.

Helen's Pattern for Healing the Pain of Loneliness

1. Eliminating self-pity.

Ask yourself: Can I take the focus of my attention off myself? Can I see my loneliness as a call from God to seek a connection with others? Can I take the energy I am using to feel miserable and use it to make someone else happy?

2. Connecting with others.

Ask yourself: Can I do some small act of kindness—send a letter, call a neighbor, make a visit—that puts me in touch with the pain of another's loneliness instead of just thinking about my own pain? Can I bring myself to remember how all the people in God's creation depend on one another? Everyone needs to feel supported and connected to others. What gifts can I contribute to healing the loneliness of the human family?

3. Experiencing connection to God.

Ask yourself: Do I talk to God regularly, not just through memorized prayers but also in friendly conversation? Can I understand that if I pray to God and I believe God hears me, then I have a unique relationship with him? Can I accept the idea that no matter what else happens in my life, if I have a relationship with God I will never be alone?

Five

Healing the Pain of Depression

Oh what a blessing to know there are reasons,
To find that each soul must, too, have its seasons—
Bounteous seasons and barren ones, too,
Times for rejoicing and times to be blue.

*A*ttempts at defining depression are not only difficult but also very risky, for the word *depression* is used variously to describe both an illness and a generalized feeling. Depression means different things to different people. One person's notion of depression may be that it is a prolonged period during which life has little meaning and less pleasure, or worse yet a black mood filled with thoughts of suicide or death. Another person might use the word to describe that sad feeling of the blues, the blahs, or a time when life temporarily loses its zest. Clearly, the gulf between the two extremes is enormous.

117

Medical science now links the *illness* of depression to genetic factors and/or biochemical imbalances. As a serious disease it requires professional medical attention and intervention. Anyone who suffers from the *illness* of depression may—indeed probably will—find encouragement that supports the healing process by reading the poetry of Helen Steiner Rice, but her inspiring words are not a substitute for medical care. In contrast, the *feeling* of depression, which may express itself as a negative state of mind or a mood of discouragement that lifts after a time, is something that we all experience at one time or another. Helen describes battles with this *feeling* of depression on many occasions throughout her life, and her strategy for defeating it was built around identifying the attitudes behind her sadness and then changing them.

Periods when she felt helpless and powerless were usually what precipitated blue moods for Helen, as they often do for all of us. Unpleasant encounters with big business, for example, triggered depression by arousing Helen's deep-seated sense of her own insignificance. She also described periods of great sadness when she contemplated the outbreak of World War II and in the years after the war, when large companies streamlined their operations and fired her friends. She felt utterly powerless at one point in the 1970s when she worried that her own employer was using her popularity to market her work without regard for her feelings. Helen also suffered regular bouts of depression each autumn when she reflected on her husband's suicide in October 1932. She always wished that she could have prevented this tragedy. As she aged, Helen felt overwhelmed by the demands of her work, and the sensation intensified as her health deteriorated.

What enabled Helen to deal with her own sadness effectively was a firm belief that even though "down" feelings were normal human emotions, she could respond to them in a constructive way. In her poems and letters Helen insisted that people should not feel guilty about having sad feelings, as they are a necessary part of being human. One way to counteract those feelings, she suggested, is to stay focused on the present, for regretting the past and fretting about what might come only fuels the feelings of sadness. If you stay in the present, you can more honestly assess any situation, accept what you cannot change, and alter the one thing you can always control—your attitude. To take this step Helen recommended replacing negative attitudes with positive thoughts. When dark thoughts arise, Helen advised, bring to mind your blessings. Developing an appreciation for even the small things we can be grateful for enables us to regain a sense of balance about our lives. Finally, Helen urged those who suffer from feelings of depression to make an effort to cheer up someone else. Giving of yourself, she promised, will bring you joy, and sadness always diminishes in the presence of joy and cheerfulness. This chapter opens with the story of Kathleen, who used Helen's poetry with amazing success in her struggle against depression.

The Story of Kathleen

Kathleen Mimms, devout Methodist Sunday school teacher and loyal member of her church choir, felt nothing but despair in the winter of 1968. A single woman of fifty-two who had practiced her faith all her life, Kathleen was diagnosed with leukemia and given only a year, two at most, to live. Even though her faith had always been an important part of her life, the devastating news made Kathleen reflect, "I guess I didn't stop to think what I really believe." She felt terribly confused, powerless, afraid, and depressed. At first she was angry at herself for feeling afraid. She said, "I shouldn't be—I know—God is close; he has always been, and yet I feel that all of a sudden he has forgotten me." Once Kathleen felt abandoned by God, she began to question whether life was worth living. Would I be better off dead? she wondered.

119

Then, in her moment of greatest fear and desperation, Kathleen happened to read the first Helen Steiner Rice poem she had ever seen, "The End of the Road Is but a Bend in the Road." The opening lines certainly captured her sentiments:

> When we feel we have nothing left to give
> And we are sure that the "song has ended"
> When our day seems over and the shadows fall
> And the darkness of night has descended . . .

Despite its ominous beginning, the rest of the poem gave her so much hope she could scarcely describe it. Could God have a bigger vision of her situation? Was it possible that everything was not as hopeless as it seemed? Could the final words of the poem really be true?

> Your work is not finished or ended,
> You've just come to a bend in the road.

Kathleen was stunned by her own reaction. She felt so much better after reading her first Helen Steiner Rice poem that she began reading everything written by Helen that she could find. When she first contacted Helen in March 1968, Kathleen's purpose was to thank her for saving her life.

> Without you and your beautiful poetry to remind me constantly of God's love, I don't know where I would be—perhaps even dead—yes even killed by my own hand. Your beautiful poetry has reminded me every hour of every day how much God cares.

Ironically it was at that darkest moment in Kathleen's life that her story of deepening faith truly began to unfold, for just as the poem she loved so much promised her, what seemed to be the end was in fact a turning point. In the spring of 1968, not long after she had written to Helen, they met, and their

120

The End of the Road Is but a Bend in the Road

When we feel we have nothing left to give
And we are sure that the "song has ended"
When our day seems over and the shadows fall
And the darkness of night has descended,
Where can we go to find the strength
To valiantly keep on trying,
Where can we find the hand that will dry
The tears that the heart is crying—
There's but one place to go and that is to God
And, dropping all pretense and pride,
We can pour out our problems without restraint
And gain strength with Him at our side—
And together we stand at life's crossroads
And view what we think is the end,
But God has a much bigger vision
And He tells us it's ONLY A BEND—
For the road goes on and is smoother,
And the "pause in the song" is a "rest,"
And the part that's unsung and unfinished
Is the sweetest and richest and best—
So rest and relax and grow stronger,
LET GO and LET GOD share your load,
Your work is not finished or ended,
You've just come to a bend in the road.

meeting uplifted Kathleen's spirits. She realized that even though she could not cure her physical disease—the recurring and spreading cancer—she could heal the way she felt and thought about it. When depression descended on her, she learned to turn to Helen and to God. When she felt a dark mood settling over her one October Sunday in 1968, she called Helen at home. Even though Helen had company, she sensed Kathleen's sadness and left her guests to spend time talking to her. What Kathleen could not have known at the time was that October, the anniversary of Franklin Rice's suicide, was a time of depression for Helen every year too.

Kathleen expressed her thanks when she wrote to Helen a few days after the phone call. She also explained that now she was consciously trying to fend off her blue moods by praying to God. She wrote, "I asked Him to forgive me for being so depressed. I promised Him that I wouldn't let myself be depressed anymore nor frightened either." It was a promise Kathleen had to struggle mightily to keep.

Helen, deeply moved by Kathleen's amazing courage in the face of continuing health problems, committed herself to helping the ailing woman conquer her dark moods. She sent Kathleen the poem "A Thankful Heart," in which she outlined her own method for combating sadness: emphasizing conscious gratitude for all the good that life offered. Kathleen welcomed the encouragement, for the advice seemed to make a real difference. For example, her spirits understandably fell when she experienced difficulty with her eyesight just as she prepared to go to the cancer center for more transfusions, but this time, rather than sinking into despair, Kathleen accepted the transitory nature of her sad feelings. She wrote frankly to Helen, "I feel like I am dying by inches. I know I sound bitter, Mrs. Rice, but I'll be fine in a few days."

Kathleen decided to use positive feelings to counter her negative ones, just as she had learned from Helen's poem. The results were most gratifying, as she happily reported:

Whenever I feel this way I pray about it and begin counting my blessings, and they outnumber my troubles. After all, I can still walk to church, I can still teach my class, I can still feel a small hand in mine, I can still hand out lollipops at the close of class, and can still be rewarded with sticky kisses.

Kathleen found that sincere gratitude and service to others helped her appreciate the present moment. When she focused on the present, she found herself humbly grateful and at peace. "I have today—this hour—this minute—this second. And for now that's all there is for anyone—what more can I ask?"

Kathleen became an inspiration to everyone around her, especially Helen Steiner Rice. The members of Kathleen's church marveled at her cheerful outlook. They never saw her battle with depression, only her good cheer and determination to live with gratitude. For her part, Helen witnessed Kathleen's transformation with awe and told her in a letter that she was so moved she spoke of her to others. "I use little incidents in our friendship and inspiring examples of your cheerfulness and courage to lift other people out of their sorrow, troubles, grief, and despair," Helen wrote and added, "You are a busy, little ministering angel to many without knowing all the good you are doing."

Despite her illness Kathleen continued to teach Sunday school and sing in her church choir; and even when the illness made her bedfast, she still managed to call others to cheer them up. While she was setting an inspiring example for those around her, Kathleen found for herself a new calm and serenity. She realized that she could not control the suffering cancer inflicted on her body, but she could control her depression, the suffering created by her mind. Perhaps more than anyone else Helen Steiner Rice ever met, Kathleen Mimms inspired her. Helen told Kathleen candidly that Kathleen had brought "a deeper sense of reality and truth" to everything Helen had ever written.

123

Helen wrote to Kathleen in March 1969 that she had been the stimulating force behind the lines in more poems than she might imagine. One was "Be of Good Cheer," which opens with words offering a lyrical description of Kathleen's attitude:

> Cheerful thoughts like sunbeams
> Lighten up the "darkest fears"
> For when the heart is happy
> There's just no time for tears.

Kathleen overcame her depression one day at a time, and Helen congratulated her, saying, "It is truly your cheerfulness that has made you healthier and happier and more loved by more people every day." Sustained by Helen's encouraging letters and poems and optimistic because of her intensified faith in God, Kathleen Mimms surpassed the doctors' prognoses by many years, even though cancer forced the removal of her jaw, most of her stomach, and one breast. She continued to correspond regularly with Helen Steiner Rice until the time of Helen's death in 1981.

In her poem "Seasons of the Soul" Helen posed a question that nearly everyone is called on to answer at one time or another:

> Why am I cast down and despondently sad
> When I long to be happy and joyous and glad?

With her own special vision, born of long experience, Helen went on to offer her personal view: Our feelings of depression and periods of sadness are really designed to lead us to deeper understanding. They symbolize the winter of the soul, or psyche; and though the seasons of the soul may not be as predictable as the seasons of nature, we all still must pass through them.

Seasons of the Soul

Why am I cast down and despondently sad
When I long to be happy and joyous and glad?
Why is my heart heavy with unfathomable weight
As I try to escape this soul-saddened state?
I ask myself often, "What makes life this way?
Why is the song silenced in the heart that was gay?"
And then with God's help it all becomes clear.
The soul has its seasons just the same as the year.
I too must pass through life's autumn of dying,
A desolate period of heart-hurt and crying,
Followed by winter in whose frostbitten hand
My heart is as frozen as the snow-covered land.
Yes, man too must pass through the seasons God sends,
Content in the knowledge that everything ends,
And oh what a blessing to know there are reasons
And to find that our soul must, too, have its seasons—
Bounteous seasons and barren ones, too,
Times for rejoicing and times to be blue,
But meeting these seasons of dark desolation
With strength that is born of anticipation
That comes from knowing the "autumn-time sadness"
Will surely be followed by a "Springtime of Gladness."

When we experience these inevitable periods of sadness, Helen suggested, it is important to keep in mind the image of winter. In wintertime everything seems cold, dead, and desolate, but in truth that barrenness is only the condition at the surface. Underneath the frozen earth new life is hard at work. Trees are preparing to bud, bulbs are poised to sprout, and nature in all its forms is getting ready to give birth to spring. And so it is with periods of sadness, said Helen. Whenever we feel dull and lifeless on the surface, we need to remember that our creativity is trapped inside, simply waiting for an opportunity to burst forth again.

According to Helen we can help ourselves discover what is waiting to emerge from our depression by asking ourselves what the sadness is about. Are we regretting the past? If so, then let it go. Give what you can do *at this moment* a chance to be born. Are you feeling worthless? Then cast off that feeling and strive to make your value to someone else emerge *now* through your acts of service. Letting go of old, "dead" attitudes so that new ones can see the light of day is the central theme of Helen's poem "Under New Management," which illustrates a vital part of her plan for healing feelings of depression:

> So if you are trying to manage your life,
> Yet all around is chaos and strife,
> Make up your mind that you too need a change
> And start making plans to somehow rearrange
> The way that you think and the things that you do
> And whatever it is that is hindering you.

Helen further understood that the discipline of living in the present worked hand in hand with what might be called "attitude management." Her poem "Put Your Soul in God's Control" is an artful summary of the virtue of focusing on the present, a practice that many medical professionals now endorse as helpful in combating stress and staving off the onset of depressive moods.

126

Under New Management

Nothing goes right—everything's wrong—
You stumble and fall as you trudge along.
The other guy wins and you always lose,
Whatever you hear is always bad news.
Well, here's some advice that's worth a try—
Businessmen use it when they want sales to soar high.
Old management goes and the new comes in,
For this is the way big business can win.
So if you are trying to manage your life,
Yet all around is chaos and strife,
Make up your mind that you too need a change
And start making plans to somehow rearrange
The way that you think and the things that you do
And whatever it is that is hindering you.
Then put yourself under God's management now,
And when He takes over you'll find that somehow
Everything changes—old things pass away
And the darkness of night becomes the brightness of
    day,
For God can transform and change into winners
The losers, the skeptics, and even the sinners.

The troubles we have suffered
Are over, past, and through,
So why should bygone happenings
Keep gravely troubling you?
And those scheduled for tomorrow
Still belong to God alone—
They are still unborn and formless
And a part of the unknown.

Helen knew from decades of experience what Kathleen Mimms learned in the course of their friendship: Thoughts can be powerful allies or deadly enemies in our efforts to defeat feelings of depression. This important message in Helen's poems dramatically changed the thinking of a Michigan woman named LoRain. She recounted the story of her own journey from depression to renewed creativity with simplicity and beauty.

The Story of LoRain

LoRain described the winter of her soul as a period of physical illness and mental depression that she could neither "shake off nor pray off." There were times, she explained, when she could not even pray for herself; all she could do was cry out for God to lay her on someone's heart. LoRain suffered from an excruciatingly painful back problem that confined her to her home and made travel out of the question. Just when things looked darkest, she received gift cards that included Helen Steiner Rice's verses. For LoRain they were a godsend. "God has met me and fed my hungry soul and sick body with the ministry of your poems," she wrote to Helen.

At that time in her life LoRain felt cut off from everything familiar; furthermore because of her disability she could no longer work outside the home. At forty-six she had to find a new way to make a living, within the confines of her walls. LoRain took stock of her assets and concluded that she needed to look at her capabilities in a new way. She decided to use her musical and artistic gifts for the benefit of others. By welcoming students into her home for piano and organ lessons and developing her talent for making ceramic figures, LoRain both brought happiness to others and satisfied her own financial needs.

Ten years later she wanted Helen to know how much her poems had provided faith, hope, and a renewed appreciation for God's love. "Today," LoRain wrote, ". . . God is still taking care of me, and in my deep gratitude I have consecrated what creative ability I have in music and ceramics to Him." Grateful for Helen's inspiration, LoRain asked for permission to send Helen a ceramic gift she created. Helen reassured the woman that her gift would be most welcome. "To put the work of your hands and the love of your heart into a creation of your own talent and skill is a true HEART GIFT," Helen replied. LoRain's spirit of giving mirrored Helen's own message perfectly, and she promised LoRain, "anything born of your own hands and heart . . . WOULD BE SURE TO PLEASE ME!"

Helen steadfastly insisted that giving one's time, energy, companionship, and love to others in acts of service or compassion helped to break the grip of depression. That sound advice, which to Helen seemed to be common sense, is now supported by numerous studies by experts whose findings indicate that altruism and voluntarism—what Helen called performing "acts of kindness"—are physically and psychologically uplifting both to the donor and the recipient. Acts of service were part of Helen's personal daily program. She wrote to her friend Mary in 1977, "I would certainly feel that my days were wasted if I did not do at least one good deed, no matter how small, in every day that passes." The substantial dividends that accrue to one's outlook from selfless giving are underscored in Helen's poem "Every Day Is a Reason for Giving—and Giving Is the Key to Living," which ends with these lines:

And he who gives of himself will find
True joy of heart and peace of mind.

Helen knew well that climbing out of a period of depression was a highly personal and very complex process. One person's ability to cope with life's blows differs vastly from another's. Helen had no professional medical training, but she understood this truth very well. She had learned it during the Great Depression, when she and her husband dealt so differently with their financial reverses. The exact circumstances that inspired Helen Steiner Rice to new creative heights drove Franklin Rice to suicide. As a result Helen knew that while she might offer someone unconditional support, each individual's capacity to benefit from her encouragement differed greatly. Ultimately, people had to find strength and answers within themselves, and sometimes, she found, that was not possible. The tragic case of Helen's friend Phil provided a grim demonstration.

The Story of Phil

Phil, like Helen, wrote greeting card verses. In addition to his job as editor for Stanley Greeting Cards in the 1940s, he contributed to *Esquire* magazine and authored the poetry segment of Walter Winchell's nationally syndicated newspaper column. He and Helen began exchanging friendly letters on professional matters, particularly their mutual need for help in their respective editorial departments, early in 1941. What began as a casual correspondence in time grew into a major source of support for Phil as he struggled through recurrent periods of deep depression.

Even in his earliest letters to Helen, Phil made little effort to conceal his feelings of worthlessness. In one of the first letters, for instance, he criticized his work for Walter Winchell as "that very bad 'Don Wahn' torch verse"; and in another he told Helen he wrote "serious stuff" too but added, "None of my efforts have been anything to write home about." Phil described writing greeting card verse during the early years of World War II as "an escape from reality."

There was, however, one bright spot in Phil's life, his two-year-old son, lightheartedly dubbed by Helen as "the young boy wonder." Sadly, the child fell ill with acute nephritis in September 1941, and Phil admitted to having been "a bit blue lately for good cause." Unfortunately, his son died in November.

Helen was quick to offer her support. She sent Phil a copy of her poem "The Master Builder," which she had written as she struggled to come to terms with her husband's death nearly ten years earlier. Phil thanked Helen profusely and wrote to her that he had immersed himself in work to ease his grief.

Just three years later Phil suffered another terrible blow. His wife and their second baby died during childbirth. Again Helen wrote offering comfort, support, empathy, and whatever assistance she could give. Phil was touched by the gesture and promised:

> I will call on you if the weight cannot be sustained by me. I am keeping your letter for good, and I will go to it when I am sorely pressed. I will take out of it your wisdom and understanding. . . . I am in your debt, for you hurried to my side in my hour of sorrow.

Reeling under these blows, Phil struggled to stay emotionally afloat. He had always been prone to melancholy, so it was that much more difficult for him to counter his sadness with positive thinking. "Rita and I had seven wonderful years marred only by the loss of our little boy," he responded to one of Helen's efforts to cheer him. He was unable to master Helen's strategy of employing faith when he was faced with crisis, characterizing himself as "a lost soul." "I puzzle and puzzle over myself," Phil wrote, "and all I get out of it is the same old self-contempt which is no answer." He realized that Helen had a kind of personal strength that he was lacking, for he wrote to Helen when her mother died at the height of World War II, "I know that the fortitude you have shown in dark moments before will come to your aid again."

Phil's natural melancholy, combined with his dreadful losses, drove him steadily downward in a spiral of depression. The severity of his condition became apparent when he suffered a nervous breakdown and then spent four months recovering in a sanitarium. Through it all, Helen continued her letters of support, comfort, and encouragement. She urged Phil to look inside himself, hoping desperately that he would find that place within where a change of attitude and healing could begin. But Phil simply could not find it. In June 1947 he wrote to Helen, "You speak of your last fifteen years. . . . I marvel at the job you have done . . . but as you say you were true to yourself. . . . My trouble is that I find no self to be true to. . . . I look inside and there's nothing there."

Despite medical treatment and Helen's support, Phil could not conquer his depression. He took his own life in March 1948.

Phil is certainly not typical of the people Helen Steiner Rice worked hard to lead through the labyrinth of depression. Phil was important to Helen, though, and she saved his correspondence among the many other letters that affirmed her skill in healing spiritual and psychological pain. Helen's friend Phil, along with her husband Franklin, stand as the two exceptions among all the people who credited her with transforming their pain into something that was elevating.

Phil and Franklin stood as graphic examples of what Helen insisted on telling others: Her words only offered a choice to an afflicted soul. Each individual had to decide whether to be overwhelmed by depression or to resist it. Every person, she knew, had a unique but often fragile capacity to resist. The following example shows how Helen's poetry in combination with professional medical support helped one man work his way through a life-threatening situation.

The Story of Jim

Jim returned home from work one day to find that his wife had left him for another man. In the months that followed he also found himself facing financial ruin, bankruptcy, and the loss of his home. Emotionally battered by so many blows, Jim became deeply depressed and admitted that he existed "in a gray and somber fog in which life became something that was unbearable and no longer worth living." Feeling he was at the end of his rope, Jim decided to end his life. He wrote a farewell letter to each of his children and left the letters on the seat of his car. Then he drove the car into the garage, shut the door, and with the engine running went to sleep. Jim's son found him two hours later, unconscious and barely alive. He rushed Jim to the hospital. When he was finally out of danger, Jim began psychiatric treatment, and while in therapy he began reading poetry.

Jim soon discovered that the faith-filled messages of Helen Steiner Rice offered a special kind of hope in his dark times. One poem, "There's Always a Springtime," he read over and over again. It led him to believe that no matter what happened, there was hope, even during this devastating winter of his soul.

> After the Winter comes the Spring
> To show us again that in everything
> There's always renewal divinely planned,
> Flawlessly perfect, the work of God's hand . . .
> God sends to the heart in its winter of sadness
> A springtime awakening of new hope and gladness.

That and other poems of Helen's helped Jim replace his despair with hope for better times. "I have started to come

There's Always a Springtime

After the Winter comes the Spring
To show us again that in everything
There's always renewal divinely planned,
Flawlessly perfect, the work of God's hand . . .
And just like the seasons that come and go
When the flowers of Spring lay buried in snow,
God sends to the heart in its winter of sadness
A springtime awakening of new hope and gladness,
And loved ones who sleep in a season of death
Will, too, be awakened by God's life-giving breath.
All who believe in God's mercy and grace
Will meet their loved ones face to face
Where time is endless and joy unbroken
And only the words of God's love are spoken.

up out of the pit that I have so long lived in," he explained, "and I believe that these books are the reason." Jim's faith in God also played a significant part in his healing. His return from the depths of hopelessness reflects the value of Helen's advice, for he found hope in the belief that "God may only be leading me to some beautiful thing that he has chosen not to reveal to me at this time." With his life turned around, Jim's experience convinced him that Helen Steiner Rice had "an unprecedented ability to communicate with those of a broken spirit."

Helen put a lot of emphasis on the necessity of faith in healing all of life's wounds. One clear difference in the stories of Phil and Jim—both of which illustrate cases of severe depression—is that Phil did not have a relationship with God, but Jim found his source of strength by returning to reliance on God. Helen felt strongly that faith was often the only thing that made life's unexpected tragedies endurable.

As Helen saw it, whenever difficulties or periods of sadness arise, faith provides all of us with the tools necessary for understanding problems from a broader perspective. Faith functions as a candle in the darkness, she wrote to her friend Gladys, but one had to be willing to let go of other supports, and that was often the hardest part: "We all feel bewildered and lonely and insecure and very frightened at times . . . but that is because we are all a little reluctant to WALK THE DARK HOURS with only the LIGHT OF FAITH to illuminate our way."

Every person confronts discouragement and sadness at different times. For some, years of thought and practice make it natural to turn to God in times of trouble; for others, the desire to rely on God is present but the feeling that depression and trouble are punishments from God make it hard to walk in faith. Doris's experience, and Willy's as well, are examples of how these kinds of struggles occur in daily life.

Never Be Discouraged

There is really nothing we need know
Or even try to understand
If we refuse to be discouraged
And trust in God's Guiding Hand . . .
So take heart and meet each minute
With Faith in God's Great Love,
Aware that every day of life
Is controlled by God Above . . .
And never dread Tomorrow
Or what the Future brings,
Just pray for strength and courage
And trust God in all things . . .
And never grow discouraged
Be patient and just wait
For "God never comes too early
And He Never Comes Too Late!"

The Story of Doris

It often seems to Doris that her problems are overwhelming. She feels that she has bad luck and is surrounded by negative people. It troubles her that those who hurt others seem to have good fortune, while her life is in turmoil. Even at bingo, laments Doris, the same people win. "Why not me? . . . I do believe in faith and hope but I also feel that I am being punished for something," she explains. Doris has begun to read the poetry of Helen Steiner Rice. She loves the poem "Never Be Discouraged," although she admits she does give up at times. These lines of the poem speak about the importance of faith:

> So take heart and meet each minute
> With Faith in God's Great Love,
> Aware that every day of life
> Is controlled by God Above.

How hard it is for Doris to trust a God she fears is deliberately hurting her! Doris's perceptions of God do not match Helen's. Helen's God is not a vengeful, punishing deity. The God Helen writes about is forgiving, compassionate, and loving. Helen's God allows trouble in our lives "to establish our CITIZENSHIP more firmly in ETERNITY." The God of Helen Steiner Rice wants us to live in faith, to "become more deeply aware that OUR TOMORROWS are in ETERNAL HANDS." Clearly our perception of God controls to some extent our ability to face and conquer sadness. It also often tells us a great deal about our outlook on ourselves and on life.

Doris has searched her soul and her life. "I know in life nothing comes smooth," she admits. She has read and reflected on the poem "Each Day Brings a Chance to Do Better." She now hopes "every day through faith and hope that things will get better with God on my side."

When Trouble Comes and Things Go Wrong!

Let us go quietly to God
When troubles come to us,
Let us never stop to whimper
Or complain and fret and fuss,
Let us hide "our thorns" in "roses"
And our sighs in "golden song"
And "our crosses" in a "crown of smiles"
Whenever things go wrong . . .
For no one can really help us
As our troubles we bemoan,
For comfort, help and inner peace
Must come from God alone . . .
So do not tell your neighbor,
Your companion or your friend
In the hope that they can help you
Bring your troubles to an end . . .
For they, too, have their problems,
They are burdened just like you,
So take your cross to Jesus
And He will see you through . . .
And waste no time in crying
On the shoulder of a friend
But go directly to the Lord
For on Him you can depend . . .
For there's absolutely nothing
That His mighty hand can't do
And He never is too busy
To help and comfort you.

Doris is trying to learn to live one day at a time despite the troubles and negativity around her. So too is Willy, who found that Helen's poetry helped him open a doorway to faith in the midst of a bleak and depressing existence.

The Story of Willy

Willy is a prisoner in a state correctional facility and is serving a life sentence. "I am only seventeen years old," he writes, "and will never be free again." Until he received Helen's poem "When Trouble Comes and Things Go Wrong!" he was deeply depressed. He was ready to commit suicide, he admits. "I was afraid to go on with my life alone." Then he read lines that changed his attitude completely:

> Let us go quietly to God
> When troubles come to us,
> Let us never stop to whimper
> Or complain and fret and fuss . . .
> For no one can really help us
> As our troubles we bemoan,
> For comfort, help and inner peace
> Must come from God alone.

That poem "brought a whole new outlook on life for me," Willy writes. The poem seemed to be a vote of confidence that his life still had meaning. Despite all the years of prison ahead of him, Willy now has faith. "Now I know that the Lord will be with me along my journey through a (hellish) life," he says.

Periods of depression and sadness hardly need such wrenchingly painful conditions as Willy's to take command of our lives. Helen herself attested to the fact that melancholy can be ushered in by many different events at any time. For example, she found herself in the middle of a season of sorrow in 1939 during what should have been a happy time, when she was vacationing abroad. However, while there she witnessed the European nations preparing in earnest for war. "I haven't felt very gay or talkative since I have been home from abroad," she wrote to her friend Alice. She tried to explain her disconcerting feelings, continuing, "We are living in a crazy-confused and insane world today and it almost seems that a sinister force is silently and slowly enveloping the entire world and crushing it to destruction and death." Helen went on to relate that sad as she felt, she refused to be dominated by despondency. She applied to herself her remedy of living in the present:

> I always try to remember the old saying—which I always find to be true if I will just keep saying it over and over—"No man ever falls under the BURDEN of TODAY—it is only when the BURDEN of TOMORROW is added to the BURDEN of TODAY that man falters—then stumbles and falls."
>
> How often we worry about TOMORROW when in reality TOMORROW never comes. For TODAY is the TOMORROW you worried about YESTERDAY.

Helen's technique of fighting negative thoughts by countering them with positive ones always lifted her spirits and has been successfully employed by many who have appreciated her clear thinking. Wilma is one who finds that this approach works.

Wilma loves Helen's poetry. Her favorite poem for focusing on the positive is "Burdens Are Things God Turns into Wings."

> If we would shoulder our daily trials
> And learn to wear them with sunny smiles
> We'd find they were wings that God had sent
> To lift us above our heart's discontent.

Whenever Wilma finds that she is feeling blue, she just reads that favorite poem and it makes her feel happy again. Wilma also

Burdens Are Things God Turns into Wings

"Oh, for the wings of a bird," we cry,
To carry us off to an untroubled sky
Where we can dwell untouched by care
And always be free as a bird in the air—
But there is a legend that's very old,
Not often heard and seldom told
That once all birds were wingless, too,
Unable to soar through the skies of blue—
For, while their plumage was beautifully bright
And their chirping songs were liltingly light,
They, too, were powerless to fly
Until one day when the Lord came by
And laid at the feet of the singing birds
Gossamer wings as He spoke these words:
"Come take these burdens, so heavy now,
But if you bear them you'll learn somehow
That as you wear them they'll grow light
And soon you can lift yourself into flight"—
So folding the wings beneath their hearts,
And after endless failures and starts,
They lifted themselves and found with delight
The wings that were heavy had grown so light—
So let us, too, listen to God's wise words,
For we are much like the "wingless birds,"
And if we would shoulder our daily trials
And learn to wear them with sunny smiles
We'd find they were wings that God had sent
To lift us above our heart's discontent—
For the wings that lift us out of despair
Are made by God from the weight of care,
So whenever you cry for "the wings of a bird"
Remember this little legend you've heard
And let God give you a heart that sings
As He turns your burdens to silver wings.

makes it a practice to cheer others by sending them uplifting messages by Helen Steiner Rice.

The poems of Helen Steiner Rice provide a reservoir of positive thoughts for people to draw on when they feel sad and troubled. Like Wilma, Marilyn has also found Helen's poems encouraging. She found that certain verses precipitated a complete transformation of attitude in her life. "I've been going through some really hard times," she writes. "I've sometimes felt like I just could not cope." Marilyn has found more love for God in her life than ever before through her renewed Christian faith and the heartening words of Helen Steiner Rice. She lives by the poem "Each Day Brings a Chance to Do Better" and has learned through her experiences, she says, that "miracles do come true if you believe."

Along with the two forms of depression discussed so far—true illness and feelings of sadness—Helen recognized a third, quite different, form of the affliction. This was spiritual depression, a singularly painful psychological experience that became a crucial part of Helen's spiritual maturation. The "dark night of the soul," as it has long been described in spiritual literature, can sweep through the life of a faith-filled person, leaving him or her feeling desolate and disoriented and suffering from an acute sense of the absence of God. Helen felt the pain of this experience to be worse than any physical discomfort, and in a letter to her friend, Sister Louise, she provided a classic description of what one endures at such a time.

> I realize these pains are so intense because I have been so blessed in always having such an AWARENESS of GOD'S PRESENCE. So whenever these periods come and I feel there is a SHADOW hiding HIS FACE from me, it is like a GREAT BEREAVEMENT and my heart is broken.
>
> It has nothing to do with FAITH, for my FAITH remains the same. It is just that I want the joy of feeling HIM near to me. But I think He sends these periods to make us realize that even though we do not have this AWARENESS, HE is with us in the SHADOWS and loving us just as much as when we can feel HIS nearness. But it is an awful struggle trying to go through these times.

Helen realized that God initiated the "dark night" and only God could lift the darkness. This spiritual rite of passage was effectively beyond human comprehension. This was one form of depression that was entirely interior, and Helen had no rhymes or sage words of advice to deal with it; she could do nothing to alleviate it. She could, however, wait patiently until the dark night gave way to a new spiritual dawn and during the interim maintain a cheerful attitude in her daily encounters with others. That is exactly what she did.

Helen believed that whether she faced spiritual depression or the more common periods of sadness and discouragement that beset everyone from time to time, she had a choice. She could choose to dwell on feelings of being helpless, powerless, and victimized or she could look for the meaning behind those feelings. Periods of depression, according to Helen, invite us to ask hard questions. Are we self-absorbed? Are we filled with self-pity or self-loathing? Do we blame our despondent moods on others? Or, instead, are we concentrating on living in the present? Are we making an effort to appreciate the daily blessings we often take for granted? Are we sharing our gifts with others? All of these choices are ours to make, argued Helen; the right choices lead to changed attitudes, peace, and contentment.

Since she was familiar with the three main forms of depression from observing friends and through personal experience, Helen was keenly aware of the limitations of her strategy for dealing with them. Mentally ill people, she knew, needed professional treatment. Those enduring the dark night of the soul had to trust in God and their own faith to see them through. Many who suffer from depression, however, are not on the extremes of the experience but fall somewhere in the middle. These are the people who have it in their power to change their situation by adopting Helen's method for overcoming the blues.

In her poem "Spring Awakens What Autumn Puts to Sleep," Helen summarized the significance of our periods of depression:

After Winter comes the Spring
To breathe new life in everything.

Episodes of sadness, Helen assured the reader, can be sources of new understanding and self-development rather than times of misery and gloom. All we need do is look on them as seasonal phases that offer the opportunity to reawaken possibilities that have momentarily been hidden from our view.

Helen's Pattern for Healing the Pain of Depression

1. Staying in the present moment.

Ask yourself: Can I keep my focus off regretting the past and worrying about the future? Can I assess what it is about my situation that I cannot change, such as the behavior of others? Can I take responsibility for what I *can* change, my own attitude?

2. Countering negative feelings with positive thoughts.

Ask yourself: When a negative thought arises, can I discipline myself to answer it with something positive about my life? Can I recall the things I am grateful for? Can I remind myself that while I may feel sad at the moment, I experienced good times before and they will return?

3. Moving out of misery and toward others.

Ask yourself: Can I shift my concentration away from my own sadness and realize that others, too, struggle with depressed moods? Can I recognize that life doesn't have to be perfect for me to smile at myself or at another? Can I break the cycle of sad feelings by bringing cheer to someone else?

Six

Healing the Pain of Disability

God, widen my vision so I may see
The afflictions you have sent to me . . .
Not as something to hate and despise
But a gift of love sent in disguise.

Our disabilities, whatever they are, challenge us in many different ways. They erode our sense of self, of wholeness, of feeling complete. In one way or another, disabilities seem at least at first glance to impair our ability to live normally, as others do. They seem confining and restricting. Helen Steiner Rice, however, believed that the notion of limitation arises from a narrow human perception of what life is meant to be. Whether we are someone who struggles daily with a disability or we assist and support an individual with a disability, Helen contended that the greatest limitation is not a physical handicap, but rather flawed understanding—a "disabled attitude."

Helen herself suffered for many years with a painful, incapacitating, and eventually disfiguring back condition. The vertebrae in her back began to crumble, her posture was impaired, and she developed a pronounced stoop. She was required to wear a cumbersome back brace in a futile effort to prevent further damage to her spine. To complicate matters, Helen developed a heart condition and shortness of breath as a direct result of the deterioration of her back. Yet when she spoke of her limitations at all, she preferred to describe them to her friends as "gifts of God's love."

In letters to those who faced a wide range of afflictions and to those who cared for disabled children, spouses, and parents, Helen proposed healing the pain of disability by viewing it symbolically, as something greater than pain, suffering, and disorientation. Our limitations are simply a part of the vocation to which we are called by God, Helen assured them. If we see our limitations as part of a divine plan that allows us to learn important life lessons, we can prevent ourselves from developing attitudes that are destructive and lead to even greater handicaps. A right attitude, Helen insisted, enables us to ask the vital questions, What can I learn from this experience? and How do I use it to do the work God has sent me here to accomplish?

"God never makes mistakes," was one of Helen's favorite adages, for she believed that if we maintain our faith in the divine plan, then we can transform what appear to be life's crosses into sources of strength and inspiration for ourselves and others. This chapter, which explores Helen's role in healing disability, begins with the inspiring story of Nancy, who has faced her physical limitations and those of other family members with faith, prayer, and the poetry of Helen Steiner Rice.

The Story of Nancy

Blue, red, and yellow yarn spills out onto the floor around the looms in Nancy Bauman's living room. She uses them to design and create doilies and placemats for her friends, gifts of love from a joyful heart. Nancy knows from personal experience the challenges of overcoming disability and she understands equally well the difficulties of caring for someone who is disabled. Nancy was born with birth defects in both of her eyes that seriously restricted her vision. In recent years doctors feared that removal of newly formed cataracts might further damage her retinas. Her husband of more than forty years also suffers from a degenerative disorder that has caused deterioration of the optic nerves in his eyes and affects his hearing as well. Herbert Bauman's condition has deprived him of both his eyesight and his hearing.

Nancy and her husband live in a mobile home, where Nancy's collection of Helen Steiner Rice poetry books—several in the large print editions—has a prominent place. The binding is coming off some of these books, she says, because she loves them so much and constantly refers to them. Nancy remembers the first poem by Helen Steiner Rice she ever received, one featured on a 1968 calendar. She was so moved by the sentiments that she wrote to Helen, and over the next few years they exchanged numerous letters. "I was one of her pen pals," Nancy recalls proudly. In 1970 Helen sent Nancy the large print edition of *Someone Cares,* a gift she still treasures today. Nancy has used Helen Steiner Rice books and

149

poems as a source of inspiration ever since her first encounter with them many years ago. From her point of view, "Helen makes a nice companion for the Bible."

Nancy has not allowed her physical limitations to disable her spirit. She worked for many years as a volunteer in the elementary school across the street from her home. In those days she gave Helen Steiner Rice's books as gifts to the teachers. When she was forced to quit her work at the school after the kindergarten teachers who had recruited her retired, Nancy felt her life was falling apart. She found herself leaning even more heavily on Helen Steiner Rice's poetry to fill the void. Lines from poems like "Help Yourself to Happiness" encouraged Nancy to recognize that happiness, as Helen always insisted, was a state of mind that was within everyone's reach.

> . . . in making others happy
> We will be happy, too,
> For the happiness you give away
> Returns to "shine on you."

Nancy began to reach out to others in a new way. She copied Helen's poems by hand and sent them to friends and relatives. "I am a poem lover," says Nancy; "I can't write poems, but I love to read good poems." She also discovered that she loves to cheer others with poetry.

Not only has Nancy contended with her own visual problems and her husband's limited sight and hearing, but she has faced the challenges of disability in other ways as well. Her only daughter suffered from severe epilepsy throughout her life. Eventually the young woman's condition reached the point where Nancy could no longer care for her, so she went to live in a women's care center. Sadly, her daughter's seizures became uncontrollable. She was hospitalized and heavily sedated in order to stop the seizures, but after a while she lapsed into a coma. Nancy's daughter died from respiratory complications in September 1992. Since neither Nancy nor her husband could drive, their access to their desperately ill daughter had been very limited. Feeling utterly helpless and frustrated beyond measure, Nancy took solace in God's love and Helen's poems. A lifelong member of the Old German Baptist Church, Nancy finds her King James version of the Bible and her Helen Steiner Rice poetry books to be her best friends. "I feel closer to God reading her work," says Nancy.

One of Nancy's favorite poems is "A Sure Way to a Happy Day," for she says, "Happiness is something we create in our mind" and contentment comes by "completing what God gives us to do." Nancy adds, "When you know God, there are no limitations." Helen Steiner Rice could not have said it better.

Helen had plenty of opportunity to practice her own advice for dealing with disability. She experienced pain in her back for years and initially dismissed it as the onset of minor arthritis. She found out in 1971, however, that what she thought was arthritic back pain was in fact a permanently injured spine, possibly the result of an earlier fall or some unnoticed spinal infection. Helen was told that two discs had disintegrated completely and that nothing could be done. The limp she had developed would be permanent, and she would never be able to lift, stoop, or raise her arms.

She had once offered her friend John this advice: "All our lives are troubled in this restless world. . . . Christ Himself lived in the midst of tempest and trouble but His inner life was a sea of glass and when the waves of life broke over Him—the great inner calm was always there."

Now she found that she had to heed her own counsel to achieve a state of inner calm. Helen was certain that God had a purpose in limiting her. She wrote to her friend Mary Jane, "No one can ever sway my thinking that GOD NEVER MAKES MISTAKES!" By then Helen had decided that her back injury had an important spiritual dimension. For one thing, it served to teach her

A Sure Way to a Happy Day

Happiness is something we create in our mind,
It's not something you search for and so seldom find—
It's just waking up and beginning the day
By counting our blessings and kneeling to pray—
It's giving up thoughts that breed discontent
And accepting what comes as a "gift heaven-sent"—
It's giving up wishing for things we have not
And making the best of whatever we've got—
It's knowing that life is determined for us,
And pursuing our tasks without fret, fume, or fuss—
For it's by completing what God gives us to do
That we find real contentment and happiness, too.

about her own vanity. She explained her thoughts on the matter to Mary Jane in a very personal letter:

> "Search me, O God, and know my thoughts" and help me to discriminate between a shattered ego and a shattered spine! . . . I know only too well that part of the disturbing and distressing shock was the realization that this limp would shatter my image, for I loved being FLEET OF FOOT . . . and I guess most females really don't want to be the Leaning Tower of Pisa or the Hunchback of Notre Dame!

Helen summarized her feelings with the words, "I am quite content with WHAT God sent."

She quietly endured the back pain for years, and as time passed, the illness in her spine worsened to the point where more discs disintegrated. Eventually Helen's rib cage slipped over her right lung, cutting off the oxygen supply and making it difficult for her to breathe. Despite this new burden, she maintained her attitude of acceptance, assuring her friend Audrey in 1974,

> You know I have been DOING BUSINESS WITH GOD for a long time, and HE has never failed me yet. And no matter how many disappointments He sends me, I know HIS BITTEREST DISAPPOINTMENTS become HIS SWEETEST APPOINTMENTS! So whatever happens will be HIS WILL, and I know that HIS GUIDING HAND will lead me through this LABYRINTH of TROUBLE that is surrounding me now.

The compression inside her chest soon led to heart problems, which even further restricted her ability to work and move. But through it all, she steadfastly looked for a spiritual dimension to make sense of her limitations in the context of her faith. She summed up her attitude in a letter to Ev, a friend of long standing:

> I continue to compound my physical problems. However, I will not go into much detail about this, for I am very satisfied and completely contented to be physically limited if I can continue

to be SPIRITUALLY WHOLE and keep in constant touch with GOD! . . .
In spite of all these little physical limitations, I accept everything
as part of my life, sent to bring me a lesson in living.

Helen's belief that physical limitations often enabled a person to grow spiritually was affirmed time and again throughout her own life experience, and it was also frequently corroborated by those who exchanged letters with her. One of the most persuasive of her correspondents was Judy, who dealt with her blindness in a way that enriched and inspired Helen.

The Story of Judy

Judy Engler lost her sight at the age of eight as the result of a brain tumor. Her first contact with Helen Steiner Rice's poetry was hearing it read during daily devotions at the home for the blind where she lived. Judy was instantly impressed and soon came to love Helen's poems so much that she asked a staff member to dictate them to her so she could write them in braille. The twenty-eight-year-old woman had sharpened her memory to the point where she could easily learn poems and pieces of literature and then recite them in performance at programs and social gatherings. Once she heard Helen's verses, Judy began to memorize her favorites and then recite them for others in hopes it would cheer and entertain them. Judy first wrote Helen in 1967, to thank her for the inspiration.

Needless to say, Judy's message touched Helen deeply. "YOU ARE A TRUE INSPIRATION for me to forge ahead even when the hills are steep and the mountains are high," Helen wrote in response to that first letter. She immediately saw a spiritual depth in Judy that many of her other acquaintances lacked and she was quick to comment on it: "I think, dear, you behold things with your SOUL that no eyes could ever see! How I wish I could be your eyes and read ALL MY VERSES TO YOU."

Judy's recitations of Helen's poems gave her tremendous satisfaction, and they also inspired her audiences. Her spiritual maturity combined with her exceptional memory made Judy an exhilarating performer. Her attitude toward life was simply uplifting to everyone who heard her. Immune to praise, she modestly explained to Helen that she had long since accepted her disability as a call from God.

There has been so much that has happened in my life and it's been a real struggle at times, but I wouldn't exchange any of it for an easier road. Each thing that happens makes me a better person for having had to deal with it. This is why I feel you must have been through a great deal yourself, because the words you write are so filled with inspiration.

So many have told me in the past few months that I am a real inspiration to them. God has let me go through a lot and I feel that if I am an inspiration then that must be why God left me here on earth.

Judy was determined to use her gifts and she believed that God through Helen Steiner Rice had provided her with a means for doing so. One of the packages of poems that Helen sent Judy contained Helen's photograph. Even though Judy could not see it herself, she had a friend describe Helen to her. Because Judy had experienced several years of normal sight before her blindness struck, she could vividly remember the details of faces. Consequently it was easy for her to see Helen in her mind's eye, which she happily reported to the poet in a letter.

Just as Helen's letters gave Judy incentive and encouragement, so she was always eager to send Helen gifts. On one occasion she wove a Scottish plaid blanket for Helen in her weaving class, and later she sent a tape recording of the poems

155

she recited. Helen was amazed by Judy's spirit and skills. In fact she wrote that Judy was less handicapped than many people with no physical disabilities:

You know, dear, THE PHYSICALLY WHOLE PEOPLE are often VERY CRIP-PLED SPIRITUALLY. And while it is very comfortable to have a strong body and no physical limitations, it is much better to have a STRONG SPIRIT that can accept and endure what God sends and keep growing in "SOUL STATURE" and making something BEAUTI-FUL out of life. You are truly an INSPIRATION, not only to me, but to everyone you contact. And I am sure that GOD is SPEAKING to me through YOU!

For her part, Judy felt that God enabled her to reach others through the medium of Helen's poems. "I have felt that God can use your verses through me just as well as on the Lawrence Welk Show. I may never be on T.V. but I do want to use my gift of being able to memorize just as much as I can," she wrote.

When Judy made plans to present "The Most Priceless Gift of Christmas" and "A Christmas Prayer" at a program for a women's group at her church, Helen applauded her faith and commitment.

You bear STRONG WITNESS to THE GREATNESS of GOD in turning hand-icaps into blessings that are FAR REACHING and WONDERFULLY INSPIR-ING, especially to people who are carrying burdens of their own that they feel are much too heavy for them to cope with. . . . You have proven to everyone that nothing is a LIMITATION when seen through GOD'S EYES!

Helen recognized in Judy a woman who had transformed her disability into a deeper experience of God's love. She found a similar level of spirit and courage in an invalid named Lorraine, whose attitude and letters to Helen portrayed her as anything but disabled!

156

The Story of Lorraine

During her professional life Lorraine Emmerson traveled extensively and planned excursions for others. But after her spine was seriously injured in an automobile accident, she found herself an invalid. Lorraine could have sunk into helpless despair when she realized that she would not be able to work and would have to depend on others, but she refused to succumb to bitterness and defeat. Instead, she rose to the challenge and chose to grow in faith.

Even before her accident, Lorraine had read and been inspired by Helen Steiner Rice's poetry and greeting cards. From her hospital bed in October 1967, she decided to call Helen. Her request was a modest one: permission to use one of Helen's verses on her own personal Christmas card. As she often had before, Helen granted the permission but she also felt some intuitive connection with this lady she had never met. Lorraine's positive spirit, as well as her sensitivity to others in spite of her own pain and physical limitations, inspired Helen.

In the months that followed, Lorraine telephoned Helen from time to time, and they had many mutually rewarding conversations; Lorraine was stimulated by Helen's ideas and sincere concern, and the poet was encouraged by the disabled woman's enthusiasm and cheerful attitude. "You delight my soul and make my heart sing," Helen wrote to Lorraine after one such long-distance dialogue. Lorraine was certain that Helen's verses transmitted God's message around the world, and she frankly told her so. And Helen assured Lorraine that she too made God visible to others, writing, "I can never thank God enough for coming to visit me in the person of Lorraine" and paying further tribute in a verse:

> You ask me how I know it's true
> That the Kingdom of Heaven abides in you . . .

Well, I've seen it there and I've heard God's voice
Each time you make MY HEART rejoice.

"You thank me for allowing you to use my verse," added Helen, "but it's I who should thank you for paying me the honor of wanting to use it."

Helen realized from the start that Lorraine's outlook on life transcended her disability. "No one could do more than you are doing no matter how they could fly around the country or make speeches," Helen encouraged Lorraine, adding,

for in your "limited world" you are campaigning for Christ in a way that we, who operate under our own power, could not equal. . . . What a lovely link you are in the chain of my life and how richly God blessed me when He brought you into my life. MIRA-CLES! MIRACLES! MIRACLES! . . . all around and about . . . too many for us to comprehend, assimilate, or ever grasp.

As it turned out, Helen was not alone in her assessment, for everyone who knew Lorraine concurred. One of her friends who received her Christmas card wrote that Lorraine was "an inspiration to all" who knew and loved her.

Not long after she began corresponding with Helen, the pain in Lorraine's back worsened, and her doctors decided that surgery was necessary to alleviate pressure on the affected nerve endings. Naturally this was a difficult time for Lorraine, and Helen urged her to look for the spiritual message in her suffering:

Each time I visit with you across the miles, I have another evidence that God is preparing you in the furnace of affliction for a more intimate and personal ministry. For when you become one of the sufferers, then and then only can you reach those WHO NEED YOU MOST . . . and you certainly seem to have the knack for doing that. So your crippled back has just provided the wings on which your soul has risen to new heights.

Unfortunately the surgery did not produce the results everyone optimistically expected. Instead of finding relief, Lorraine had to contend with terrible news: She would never walk again and in all likelihood would have to spend the rest of her life flat on her back, alternating between a stretcher and a rocking bed. Lorraine faced the news with determination and courage. She shared the prognosis with Helen, writing, "This, however, does *not* mean I will have to be confined to bed. I'll be able to get around the hospital on a stretcher and out on the terrace when a little warmer weather sets in. I may be 'down' but they'll *never* get me 'out,' Helen."

Typically, the purpose of Lorraine's letter was selfless. She wanted neither to complain nor to elicit sympathy, but rather simply to know if Helen would autograph booklets of prayers for volunteers at the hospital.

Since Lorraine's breathing was compromised by her back problems, she was moved to a respiratory care facility. While there, she continued to correspond with Helen, once letting her know that she had a chance to share one of Helen's poems with a young disabled woman who "really needed some cheering up." Helen was amazed at Lorraine's continued faith and good spirits and told her so:

> I think what is most marvelous about all this is your avid interest and responsive willingness to always TRY JUST ONE MORE TIME! What a witness you are for this GREAT, BIG WONDERFUL GOD! You have made your physical prison a real pulpit from which you daily bear witness to the POWER of GOD to keep one faithful, in spite of all afflictions, handicaps, and infirmities!

Very much like Judy, Lorraine exemplified extraordinary heroism in transcending her disability. Helen never could quite put into words how much regard she had for Lorraine; the best she could do was congratulate her for doing "exactly what

GOD asks all His workers to do . . . and that is to accept their cross and bear it without complaining."

You keep on serving HIM no matter in what situation you find yourself or under what conditions HE places you. There is a job for everyone to do, and when God assigned your job to you, you really GOT HIS MESSAGE! In spite of your handicap, you have proved, in whatsoever surroundings we are placed, it is possible to serve GOD!

Just as it was for Judy and Lorraine, serving God despite limitations was also the principal goal of Eileen, another disabled lady who corresponded with Helen Steiner Rice during the 1960s.

The Story of Eileen

Like Judy, Eileen had suffered from a brain tumor when she was a child. When surgery was performed to remove the tumor, it first seemed to leave Eileen completely blind and handicapped on the right side of her body. As time passed, however, Eileen regained part of the vision in one eye, which enabled her to learn touch typing with one hand in school. It delighted her to be able to type copies of Helen's poems and send them to people she knew needed encouragement. Eileen had discovered Helen's verses on greeting cards, and then she heard Helen's poems read on the Lawrence Welk Show. Her appetite whetted, she was eager to have more.

When Eileen wrote to Helen Steiner Rice in July 1962, she wanted to know if Helen had published a book that contained all of her poems. Helen quickly responded to Eileen's inquiry, and the two began to correspond. Eileen was thrilled at the prospect of exchanging messages with someone she regarded as a role model. "As I read your letter, I felt as if I've known you all my life," she wrote to Helen. "My mother and I had tears in our eyes as we read your spiritual letter and poems."

Eileen revealed that her faith in God strengthened her. She attributed her survival from the brain surgery to God's loving care and the prayers of her mother and friends. "Although I'm still handicapped in my right arm and leg from the operation, I thank God for what he has given me," she told Helen.

The thing that distressed Eileen the most at that time was her inability to find steady employment. Despite assistance from the local center for the blind, there seemed to be absolutely no job opportunities for her. She expressed her concern and frustration to Helen: "I know with my handicap it isn't easy to find something, but I keep hoping and praying that someday, somewhere, I'll find a suitable job. I know I should be patient and let God take care of it but sometimes it's hard."

Meanwhile Eileen worked at home, making jewelry to sell and she played bingo at a local hospital each week with wheelchair patients. But she remained troubled over what the future held and confided to Helen that her poems had truly helped. "When a person is so depressed and doesn't know where to turn, a spiritual poem, like yours, can sometimes show them the way, far better than a preacher could ever explain," she wrote.

There were times, Eileen explained, when she wondered whether there really was a place in the world for her because she had neither a college education nor "high position." Yet she told Helen about another time when she was feeling blue and the thought came to her, *There's a much higher college, the spiritual college, in which we must learn love, kindness, patience, and understanding for each other.* This thought helped Eileen realize, despite her discouragement, "that when you've learned this kind of knowledge, college and high position mean very little."

Helen kept providing inspiration, encouragement, and poetry by mail. She also prayed that God would send Eileen the right job, and she sent her a supply of Christmas cards.

161

Eileen was elated. "I've never seen or read such beautiful Christmas cards!" she exclaimed to Helen. Eileen was so taken by the gesture that she had a friend print copies of Helen's poems and sent out five hundred of them! "It might not be much," Eileen wrote to Helen, "but if only a few souls start thinking about God, it was worth all the work and effort."

In January 1963 a delighted Eileen wrote to Helen, "God sure must listen to your prayers!" She had finally found a job. A former high school teacher to whom Eileen had sent one of Helen's poems got in touch with her to say thanks and asked if she would like a job at a nearby library. She began training to type reference cards and started working with a woman who had survived polio and consequently understood what it was like to be handicapped. "If it wasn't for your poems, this wouldn't have happened," Eileen gratefully reported to Helen. "Thank you again for all your beautiful poems and nice thoughts."

Eileen and Helen Steiner Rice corresponded for more than fifteen years. Helen's poems and letters seemed to arrive at exactly the times when Eileen needed a lift. "May God repay you for your thoughtfulness," Eileen once wrote. "There are so many people with all kinds of problems, and your poems will come as a ray of light shining through the darkest cloud."

Helen's poems certainly offer the ray of light Eileen described, not only to the disabled, but also to those who face the task of caring for a handicapped child or relative. The same attitudes that make it possible for healing to begin in a person who is disabled also work for those who support and sustain such an individual. Helen's correspondence with a New Hampshire mother is a perfect case in point, for it reveals how this woman matured as she accepted the call to care for her child, learned from her own limitations, and looked for God's purpose in the life of her son.

The Way to God

If my days were untroubled
And my heart always light
Would I seek that fair land
Where there is no night;
If I never grew weary
With the weight of my load
Would I search for God's Peace
At the end of the road;
If I never knew sickness
And never felt pain
Would I reach for a hand
To help and sustain;
If I walked not with sorrow
And lived without loss
Would my soul seek sweet solace
At the foot of the cross;
If all I desired was mine
Day by day
Would I kneel before God
And earnestly pray;
If God sent no "Winter"
To freeze me with fear
Would I yearn for the warmth
Of "Spring" every year;
I ask myself this and the answer is plain—
If my life were all pleasure
And I never knew pain
I'd seek God less often and need Him much less
For God's sought more often
In times of distress,
And no one knows God
Or sees Him as plain
As those who have met Him
On "The Pathway of Pain."

The Story of Marion

Marion became alarmed when her youngest child, two-year-old Mark, failed to develop as her other children had. "He seemed to be living in his own little world," she recounted, "and could not even say mamma." Tests at a nearby children's medical center confirmed her devastating suspicion: the child was deaf. To comfort Marion at this difficult time, a friend sent her one of Helen Steiner Rice's greeting cards that included the verse "The Way to God." It described the central role of life's burdens in drawing one closer to God.

> If I never grew weary with
> The weight of my load
> Would I search for God's Peace
> At the end of the road . . .
> If all I desired was mine
> Day by day
> Would I kneel before God
> And earnestly pray . . .

Other friends sent Marion more of Helen's poems and cards, and in each one the grieving lady found strength and a new perspective. She finally wrote a thank-you letter to Helen in September 1966, giving voice to her gratitude. "Words cannot express how much your poems have helped me," she wrote.

Marion's personal heartache and the disappointment she felt for her son were compounded by frustration with herself. She felt so discouraged with her own limitations, by her inability to solve the problem and make the situation better. Then she read these words from Helen's poem "On the Wings of Prayer":

> But God only asks us to do our best,
> Then He will "take over" and finish the rest.

On the Wings of Prayer

Just close your eyes and open your heart
And feel your worries and cares depart,
Just yield yourself to the Father above
And let Him hold you secure in His love—
For life on earth grows more involved
With endless problems that can't be solved—
But God only asks us to do our best,
Then He will "take over" and finish the rest—
So when you are tired, discouraged and blue,
There's always one door that is open to you—
And that is the door to "The House of Prayer"
And you'll find God waiting to meet you there,
And "the House of Prayer" is no farther away
Than the quiet spot where you kneel and pray—
For the heart is a temple when God is there
As we place ourselves in His loving care,
And He hears every prayer and answers each one
When we pray in His name "THY WILL BE DONE"—
And the burdens that seemed too heavy to bear
Are lifted away on "THE WINGS OF PRAYER."

"What a comforting thought this brings to mind," she wrote to Helen. "God is in control—I only have to do my best—I don't have to exhaust myself trying to do the impossible. Yes, Mrs. Rice, your poem helped to make me become more mature."

Helen responded as soon as she received Marion's poignant letter. "My dear," she began, "letters such as yours are my rich reward direct from the Lord." She hastened to assure Marion that her child gave divine purpose to Marion's life. "God makes bright crowns from HEAVY CROSSES and little Mark was sent to you not as a CROSS but a STAR for YOUR CROWN," she wrote.

Subsequently Helen's poems became part of daily life for Marion and her family. Marion began to use the poems as devotional guides to lead her to Bible passages. Her husband, a physical therapist, carried Helen's poems with him to give to clients who were discouraged with their own handicaps. Marion's older children gave her Helen Steiner Rice's books for Mother's Day presents. Over the next few months doctors discovered that Marion's son suffered from multiple handicaps, but by then Marion had found peace with herself and had come to terms with the role God was asking her to play. She later wrote to Helen about the transformation in her attitude regarding Mark's disability:

> I used to feel that if only he could say Mamma or Dadda, . . . but now I realize that God's will is much more important than my selfish desires. . . . Mark is in his hands and that is the main thing. All other things will fall into place. Reading your poems, the Bible, and praying has made me realize this. Yes, Mrs. Rice, I'm meeting each day with complete confidence that God will solve the problems over which I have no control.

Another mother who found solace in Helen's poetry wrote to ask if Helen would write a special poem that could be used at the dedication of the Resident Home for the Mentally Retarded in Cincinnati in 1967. This woman, whose three-year-old daughter, Lisa, was mentally handicapped, had found inspiration in

Helen's verses and she graphically outlined for Helen the pain each family faces when presented with such a challenge.

The Story of Nola

Nola believed that God shared special lessons with her family through the presence of a handicapped child, despite the moments of discouragement. One thing Nola had learned from caring for Lisa was acceptance. She had also learned how important it is for parents who struggle with similar situations to support one another. Helen Steiner Rice's messages that every experience serves to further God's plan and that kindness between people transforms lives convinced Nola that Helen could reach the families of mentally handicapped children in a profound way.

The main question that every family with a mentally impaired child asked, Nola explained in a letter to Helen, is why? "They wonder why God allowed this to be brought on them. Some feel guilty, some ashamed, and some feel like it is a punishment." Even though the why may never be answered, Nola continued, support groups enable parents to understand "how the living God can enable them to live serenely in difficult circumstances." The Resident Home for the Mentally Retarded took into its training center children who could not be assimilated into any special education classes. Some suffered from Down's syndrome and some were brain damaged; others exhibited unmanageable behavior. "Always the parents need someone to help them see that this is a life-shaking experience; it need not be life-breaking," Nola wrote. She felt that a poem written by Helen, who had inspired so many others, could provide the words these parents needed to hear and would make the dedication booklet complete.

In response to Nola's request Helen composed the poem "Blessings in Disguise Are Difficult to Recognize." The lines

167

Blessings in Disguise Are Difficult to Recognize

God sends His "little angels"
In many forms and guises,
They come as lovely miracles
That God alone devises—
For He does nothing without purpose,
Everything's a perfect plan
To fulfill in bounteous measure
All He ever promised man—
For every "little angel"
With a body bent and broken,
Or a little mind retarded
Or little words unspoken,
Is just God's way of trying
To reach and touch the hand
Of all who do not know Him
And cannot understand
That often through an angel
Whose "wings will never fly"
The Lord is pointing out the way
To His eternal sky
Where there will be no handicaps
Of body, soul or mind,
And where all limitations
Will be dropped and left behind—
So accept these "little angels"
As gifts from God above
And thank Him for this lesson
In FAITH and HOPE and LOVE.

of that poem were written specifically to encourage parents to find the wisdom of God through "little angels," like Nola's Lisa, "whose wings will never fly."

The theme of "Blessings in Disguise" was also the focal point of a letter Helen wrote to Karen, the daughter of a friend.

The Story of Karen

Karen's baby was born with a birth defect. Helen shared her feelings with Karen when she heard the news:

> I was filled with mixed emotions . . . GLADNESS because this little fellow was surrounded with a loving mother and father and grandmother and then SADNESS that there were some UNCERTAIN HOURS OF ANXIETY that had entered into your newfound happiness.

Helen encouraged the new mother to place her child in God's hands and to have faith. "God sends us many disappointments, but He sends them to us as blessings in disguise, and He is really sending them to us so that we may grow in grace and better understand the miracles that He can do," she wrote.

Certainly Evelyn, who was a devoted collector of Helen Steiner Rice's cards, believed she had grown in grace as the result of her experience with her foster child. She wrote to Helen with humor and humility.

The Story of Evelyn

Evelyn was so dedicated in searching for and buying every card and booklet by Helen Steiner Rice that she became known as "the little HSR lady" in her small town in England. But Evelyn's life did not revolve entirely around her devotion to Helen's work. She was even more committed to caring for her foster son, a little boy who was lame and tormented by behavioral problems. There was, however, a very close connection between these two enthralling points of Evelyn's life, for Helen's verses helped her see what a gift this child had been to her family. "Having Laurence has brought us closer together," Evelyn wrote to Helen, "for bringing him up has not been easy and so it has needed a combined family effort which has taught us to be more tolerant and understanding amongst ourselves and towards other people." Evelyn knew the wisdom in Helen's poem "Before You Can Dry Another's Tears You Too Must Weep," for its lines neatly expressed both the problems and solutions of her life.

> So spare me no heartache or sorrow, dear Lord,
> For the heart that is hurt reaps the richest reward,
> And God enters the heart that is broken with sorrow
> As He opens the door to a Brighter Tomorrow.

Despite the heartaches and challenges Laurence presented, Evelyn nonetheless found him to be a source of great joy. He attended a Saturday morning club for the handicapped at their parish church and always seemed eager to attend the Mass that was part of the program. Evelyn described to Helen Laurence's effort to recount the prayers he heard; it led Evelyn to smile in private amusement: "As he is a very naughty little boy at times you can imagine how funny it is when he says, 'O Lord, I am not *worth* it,' instead of 'O Lord, I am not *worthy* . . . , and 'Lead me not into the *station*' instead of 'Lead me not into *temptation.*'" Helen wrote back, assuring Evelyn that God was listening to Laurence's prayers "no matter how he mixes them up." Evelyn agreed.

Evelyn believed that Laurence had come to her as part of God's way of opening her heart in compassion. In spite of his twisted legs and his emotional problems, Laurence was happy with life just as it is. "Without him," Evelyn reckoned, "I would never have been the person I am today. I was so hard and unemotional. . . . I had put up some sort of barrier against the world and it has taken Laurence to break this down."

Like Evelyn, Helen believed that the disabilities we struggle with—either our own or those of others we care about—are God's way of breaking down our barriers, of forcing us to look for a divine order that transcends human logic, of drawing us closer to the divine and to one another. As her own back condition worsened, Helen wrote to a friend, "I feel in my heart that, in spite of all the pain I am enduring, GOD CHOSE ME to suffer so that I might better understand the suffering of others." Her own disability made Helen feel the "touch of God," and she referred to it as her "testing ground," an experience that challenged her to grow in patience and faith. From Helen's vantage point her physical impairment appeared to be a source of spiritual enrichment: "I feel that each day that hampers me in my daily pursuits strengthens my soul, and so with this I am going to try to content myself even though the struggle is almost overpowering."

In the end, Helen followed with grace and faith the advice she gave to others who suffered from physical limitations. She put her feelings this way when she wrote to a friend in 1976 after being hospitalized and fitted with a back brace,

> I am accepting this all as THE GREATEST GIFT GOD ever sent to me. . . .
> I have always been very impatient about everything, and this is
> making me aware that if I want to be a true disciple of THE LORD, I
> must take up my cross and follow HIM, for no one belongs on GOD'S
> ROAD if he has no cross to carry.

She found divine purpose, saying, "I realize only HIS LOVE and WISDOM could have known I needed this brace not only for MY BACK but for MY SOUL." In dealing with disability as with everything else, Helen Steiner Rice taught what she knew. For her, disability was a gift of love in disguise.

Helen's Pattern for Healing the Pain of Disability

1. Accepting God's call.

Ask yourself: Do I understand that every person is called by God to face different kinds of challenges and accept various limitations? Do I understand that I am whole in God's eyes and lacking nothing for the task to which I have been called by the Almighty?

2. Learning from limitations.

Ask yourself: Am I aware that a disabled attitude is far more limiting than a disabled body? Am I aware that my physical limitations enable me to develop other abilities to a heightened degree? What has my limitation taught me that will help me be more compassionate toward others?

3. Finding divine purpose and meaning in life.

Ask yourself: Do I recognize that my life has purpose and I have a gift to share with this world? Do I realize that my limitation may be the means through which I will be able to express my gift? Can I accept my life—exactly as it is—as a gift of God's love? Can I think of my limitation as a way to experience the presence of God in my life more completely?

Seven

Healing the Pain of Infirmity

For God who sets our span of years
And watches from above
Replaces youth and beauty
With peace and truth and love.

The final years of life force us to make adjustments at every turn. While retirement may herald life's golden years for some, for just as many or more it ushers in health problems, physical limitations, financial strain, and dependence on others. Sometimes it does not seem that "peace and truth and love" come as the reward for growing older. And yet Helen Steiner Rice believed that all the difficulties of the later years of life are God's way of refining the soul as it moves toward its divine destiny. The secret to peace, she resolutely believed, is not resistance but acceptance.

How hard it was for Helen to accept the changes of her later years! The demands on her time increased as her health deteriorated, and she felt terribly frustrated because there was so much she wanted to do. She particularly hated the idea of slowing down. Even though Helen officially retired as editor at Gibson Greetings in 1971, she continued for years to write poetry and correspond with her many friends and legions of fans. As if her life was not complicated enough during her final decade, she was evicted from her home of forty years at the Gibson Hotel and forced to relocate. But perhaps the most difficult adjustment of all was that her failing health made Helen completely dependent on others to get to church, go to her office, and attend social gatherings. And then, at the age of eighty, she broke her hip and spent her last days confined to a nursing home. Nonetheless, Helen managed to age with grace, and her approach to dealing with the challenges of her declining years provides a model for healing the pain of aging and infirmity.

Her letters during these final years make it clear that Helen experienced all the disturbing emotions accompanying the pain, frustration, dislocation, and limitations of growing older. They also illustrate how she transformed these experiences, choosing—instead of self-pity and regret for lost youth—a path to serenity. Along the way as she coped with her own problems, Helen also found the strength to encourage others to face the aging process with cheerfulness and faith and to understand it as a time to develop spiritual maturity.

Helen realized that God offered her a choice during her final years. She could resist the inevitable transitions of aging and infirmity and become bitter and complaining, or she could accept each encounter God sent her as a means of uniting her will to that of God, whom she had professed to serve her whole life. In every act of surrender, Helen found the peace that healed the pain of infirmity. This chapter opens with the story of Ruth, who found peace in infirmity with the help of Helen Steiner Rice's poetry.

The Story of Ruth

Ruth Keefe's son once made a drawing of the familiar advertising character the Energizer Bunny around her picture, because she has "kept on going" with energy and good cheer despite a twenty-two-year battle against cancer. Ruth liked it so much she used the bunny drawing on a luncheon invitation she sent to her friends. It was an appropriate gesture, for to everyone who knows her, Ruth has become a symbol of someone who never gives up.

When she was first diagnosed with cancer in 1974, doctors prescribed surgery and cobalt treatments. The cobalt treatments left her with nerve damage and severe, unrelenting pain. In addition to all of her suffering, the cancer returned six times over a period of two decades. By 1987, when Ruth's doctors discovered non-Hodgkin's lymphoma, routine CAT scans had become a mandatory procedure in monitoring the disease. It only made things worse for Ruth, for the contrast dye she had to drink before the tests made her violently ill. During the initial treatments Ruth simply put up with the nausea, vomiting, and intestinal cramping caused by the dye in her system. Her response was so predictable that when she arrived at the hospital, she was given a chair near the bathroom. Then a gift from a longtime friend changed everything. Ruth received a book of Helen Steiner Rice's poems.

Many years before, Ruth had been a bridesmaid in the wedding of Virginia Ruehlmann, the administrator of the Helen Steiner Rice Foundation. Since she was familiar with Ruth's

Believe

When the way seems long and the day is dark
And we can't hear the sound of the thrush or the lark,
That is the time when faith alone
Can lead us out of the dark unknown.
For faith to believe when the way is rough
And faith to hang on when the going is tough
Will never fail to pull us through
And bring us strength and comfort, too.
For all we really ever need
Is faith as a grain of mustard seed,
For all God asks is do you believe—
For if you do you shall receive.

difficulties, Virginia thought Ruth might find comfort in some of Helen's poems. As it turned out, Virginia's guess was accurate. Ruth, who is a woman of great faith, began to read the poems and prayers in the little book *Wings of Encouragement.* One of Ruth's favorite poems is "Believe." In it Helen assured her readers that "faith alone" is sufficient to comfort and strengthen us when "the day is dark" and "the way is rough." Ruth suddenly realized that Helen's writings were giving her far more than either she or Virginia had expected; it was "a physical lift, not just an emotional one." Ruth started taking the book with her to the hospital, and the effect was transforming. If she read Helen Steiner Rice's poems while drinking the contrast dye, she no longer became ill. The cramping, the nausea, and all the other terrible effects on her body subsided. Ruth concluded that Helen's poetry made the CAT scan ordeals much more tolerable because the verses had "a medicinal benefit."

Ruth knows herself well and she believes that her attitude, in addition to Helen's encouraging words, makes all the difference in the world when it comes to healing the pain of infirmity. Now in her seventies, she has remained active despite the cancer and the treatments that have kept it at bay. She recently chaired two fund-raisers to benefit local religious communities, and she meets regularly with the Catholic Visitation Society to sew baby layettes. "If you are active, you don't notice the pain so much," Ruth affirms. She also uses the technique known as guided imagery to soothe her spirit and her body. Among the powerful images she uses is one of a fire brigade composed of her favorite saints. In her mind's eye she watches them hose down her body with a foam that destroys the cancer cells. "I know it works," she declares, and the fact that she is doing so well supports her testimony.

At the local Wellness Center Ruth is a loyal participant in a cancer support group, a powerful and positive experience for her. Her friends there help her celebrate not only her life, but also her limitations. They realize that sometimes just getting

177

dinner on the table is an accomplishment for Ruth, and they applaud it. The group also encourages joking and good humor, even if sometimes it is black humor. Their laughter helps them deal openly with their mutual struggle against cancer, and the support is a healing and effective medicine.

Above all, Ruth subscribes to Helen Steiner Rice's conviction that experiencing peace ultimately comes from having faith in God's higher plan. She has seen many who are without faith, and for them the prospect of death is terrifying. "If you have faith," Ruth says, "you're not afraid of dying." In her daily acceptance of herself and her limitations, her sense of humor and cheerfulness, and her surrender in faith to God's great plan, Ruth offers a fine example of Helen Steiner Rice's pattern for healing the pain of infirmity. Ruth understands as she ages that God has replaced many of the treasures of her younger years with the more precious ones of peace and truth and love.

Helen's poems and advice on infirmity strike such a responsive chord in others because she understood that while all of life was a gradual letting-go experience, in one's final years the need to let go intensifies. Letting go, according to Helen, means slowly abandoning one's personal agenda and accepting a divine agenda. It is usually a confusing, painful, and mysterious process. Aging and infirmity are not curses or afflictions, but rather way stations on the road home to God. They prepare one for the time of final letting go and serve as an invitation to surrender everything but faith in God's love.

It is interesting that Helen, being the astute observer of human nature that she was, became aware of the pattern for healing infirmity long before she was required to address the matter herself. As a result, examples of her advice to those who were aged and ailing date back many years before she began to consider herself a senior citizen. One who benefited from Helen's encouragement in the early 1960s was her friend Goebel.

The Story of Goebel

For years Goebel worked as a bellman at the Gibson Hotel, where Helen lived. Virtually from the moment they first met, Goebel noticed Helen's kindness, her good cheer, and her courtesy, and he was especially impressed by her gracious practice of treating everyone with respect and friendliness. Goebel delighted, for instance, in the fact that Helen Steiner Rice, the famous poet, called him "Mr. Thompson." Helen rarely failed in her efforts to make people feel good about themselves.

Goebel suffered from tuberculosis, and when the disease worsened in the summer of 1963, he was admitted to a TB hospital in Kentucky. Predictably, Helen made it her business to find out where Goebel was convalescing. She sent him a letter of encouragement and a package of inspirational poems, "the most wonderful gift and letter," Goebel wrote, that he had ever received.

The elderly man wanted Helen to know how much her friendship and concern had meant to him, particularly in his time of debilitating illness. He described for Helen the scene at the TB sanitarium when one Saturday night the Lawrence Welk Show came on the television in the common room and Helen's name and the title of her poem were announced, as Goebel put it, "to millions of their viewers":

> To think an old bellman in a TB hospital can get up and shout, "That lady who you speak of is my friend and the friend to so many bellmen and people it would take the hour show for a fellow like me to tell the world just what a person Mrs. Rice really is. I mean a lady who commands respect, is respected, and respects each person regardless of race, color, religion, or anything one can think of."

Helen's letters buoyed Goebel's spirits and he wrote to her again, searching for the right words to express "the real mean-

179

ing and the help" she had been to him and to others in the hospital "that may never get to know or see a Great Lady like you. . . ."

Goebel knew he felt better because of Helen's interest in him and concern for his well-being, but one thing puzzled him. He confided to Helen, "I have tried and have asked others who I respect and I know who use good judgment just why would a lady of your many talents . . . show such an interest in a bellman, and not only me but thousands of people."

A nurse at the hospital gave Goebel the answer he was searching for, and he passed it along in his next letter to Helen.

"Goebel," she said, "don't you think God has his helpers at work in all walks of life where others would tire? Mrs. Rice gets blessings, graces, and help to carry on the work she is so suited to do. . . . Her mission is to let you and all she comes in contact with know how easy it is to be good and at the same time respect your fellow men."

Goebel insisted that if he was as considerate and cooperative a patient as Helen gave him credit for being, it was because some of her courtesy and kindness rubbed off on him in the lobby of the Gibson Hotel.

On his release from the hospital, Goebel took all his Helen Steiner Rice poems home. One in particular brought about a transformation of attitude in his household. It was "The Legend of the Raindrop," which told of the value of even the stormy days of life. One rainy Monday morning Goebel's wife, Mary, told him the verses had inspired a change of heart in her: "On Mondays past, I would be complaining about those raindrops because they interfered with my wash day, but now I have learned to appreciate them just like the sun that dries my wash." Goebel assured Helen of his prayers and promised to ask God to bless her so she could continue to "put words together for folks like us to understand."

Just one year later those words Helen Steiner Rice "put together" so well helped an elderly woman transform her experience of infirmity into a faith-filled story of acceptance.

The Story of Margaret

At the age of eighty-one Margaret Burritt had four operations to delay the spread of cancer in her jawbone. She had always been an active, jovial woman, she explained in a letter to Helen. When the doctor learned her real age, he was amazed; he thought she did not look a day over sixty-five. Margaret kept house in an apartment she shared with her niece, and even though she harbored great fear about her future, she was careful never to reveal it. "Seldom speak of this condition except when it speaks too loud," she confided to Helen. When she wrote in August 1964 to thank Helen for a packet of her poems and a note of encouragement, Margaret announced she had just learned that more surgery would be necessary to contain the spread of her cancer. As might be expected, she was apprehensive.

Supportive as usual, Helen continued sending letters regularly to Margaret and reinforced her messages with poems of inspiration. One of Margaret's favorites, "So Swift the Way! So Short the Day!" arrived not long after the new round of surgery had been scheduled. It helped immensely in easing the transition from a life that had once been extremely busy into a time of reliance on God.

> Why are we impatient and continually vexed,
> And often bewildered disturbed and perplexed?

181

Perhaps we're too busy with our own selfish seeking
To hear the dear Lord when He's tenderly speaking.

Helen's message that slowing down can allow one to hear the voice of God more clearly found a welcome place in Margaret's receptive heart. Almost by magic "So Swift the Way" and other poems opened Margaret to new insights:

I have sat by the hour reading and rereading them—finding there really are God's people in this world, doing work that takes our thoughts so vividly to our Redeemer—no one can deny feeling his presence. If one is just about to give up courage in meeting unspeakable conditions—just read your poems. . . . How I love you, Darling, for the wonderful help and inspiration you have sent me at this time.

Helen's encouraging words and heartening verses undoubtedly helped Margaret along the road to spiritual healing, but their effect did not end there. They seemed to have a physical impact as well. One of her doctors pronounced the post-surgical healing of her face "Terrific!" Another, who was understandably fascinated by results that apparently had nothing to do with science, wanted to know what church she attended. Margaret was convinced that the support of her friends and Helen's writings "did the whole healing." The truth of the matter is that over the months of her illness Margaret had grown in faith and friendship with God. Helen's letters and poems gave her a new and more deeply spiritual outlook on life. She expressed it best in a letter of gratitude to Helen:

Helen, you have given me true knowledge of God [and] his aids who have brought me through my suffering in recovery. The doctors marvel at the healing I am having and are so excited and thrilled. All due to you showing me the true way of speaking with

God and knowing him. . . . How wonderful and relaxing to know One is by your side taking care—giving rest and sleep—without medication.

Over the next six months the tumor in Margaret's jawbone slowly disappeared, and at the same time her new attitudes strengthened and flourished. "Honey," she informed Helen, "had God not introduced me to you, my sickness would have been terrible. You have guided me through every mountain." By June of 1965 Margaret was able to describe how, with Helen Steiner Rice's help, her spirit had been transformed because of her infirmity. Margaret's faith continued to sustain her, she maintained a cheerful outlook, and perhaps most importantly she accepted with profound thanksgiving God's plan for her.

You have given me everything—kept me going with faith and courage no one else could direct. . . . I ask and God sends this aid to be with me. I receive faith and quietness and sleep without medical aid. All gives me such peace of mind. No one knows how my heart has ached until reading your messages. God comes to me and stills my troubles. . . .

I can be happy and cheerful—because of the help and direction you have given me. My distress and agony has ceased. I am gaining health and strength enough to continue active living. . . . God is with me and I accept all he gives with great gratitude.

Helen realized that when she surrendered her will to God, many of her illusions would be dismantled, and one by one she watched them reduced to rubble. For example, she had to abandon the notion that she had limitless energy to pour out to others. The opening lines of her poem "Give Me the Contentment of Acceptance" describes her state of mind in December 1967 as she contemplated her limitations.

Give Me the Contentment of Acceptance

In the deep dark hours of my distress
My unworthy life seems a miserable mess—
Handicapped, limited, with my strength decreasing
The demands on my time keep forever increasing
And I pray for the flair and the force of youth
So I can keep spreading God's light and His truth
For my heart's happy hope and my dearest desire
Is to continue to serve You with fervor and fire
But I no longer have strength to dramatically do
The spectacular things I loved doing for You
Forgetting entirely that all You required
Was not a "servant" the world admired
But a humbled heart and a sanctified soul
Whose only mission and purpose and goal
Was to be content with whatever God sends
And to know that to please You really depends
Not on continued and mounting success
But in learning how to become *less and less*
And to realize that we serve God best
When our one desire and only request
Is not to succumb to worldly acclaim
But honoring ourselves in Your Holy Name—
So let me say *no* to all flattery and praise
And quietly spend the rest of my days
Far from the greed and the speed of man
Who has so distorted God's simple life plan . . .
And let me be great in the eyes of the Lord
For that is the richest, most priceless reward.

Healing the Pain of Infirmity

> In the deep dark hours of my distress
> My unworthy life seems a miserable mess—
> Handicapped, limited, with my strength decreasing
> The demands on my time keep forever increasing.

That month Helen had been scheduled for three days of autograph shows in Atlanta, but exhaustion and a weakened, enlarged heart forced a change in her plans. Her doctor sent her to bed, and the promotional tour was canceled. Even under those traumatic circumstances she was able to reflect on the meaning behind the experience, searching for spiritual insight. She found what she was looking for and revealed it in a letter of empathy to Aladdin Pallante, a performer on the Lawrence Welk Show, who had himself recently suffered a heart attack.

> I was floating on clouds with wings on my heels until God stepped in and curtailed all this *"self-glorification."* . . . Looking back it was the most wonderful gift God ever sent me but when it came it was wrapped so unattractively that I refused to accept it as a gift. . . . Now I regulate my schedules and can see it was sheer folly to dissipate my endurance and vitality so recklessly, and I now realize that God always gives us strength to do WHAT HE MOST WANTS US TO DO but we throw in the extra to delight ourselves.

Helen also tailored the message of one of her latest poems for Aladdin, but it was a message she realized she too needed to heed.

> Sometimes the things that seem the WORST
> turn out to be the BEST . . .
> And this is just a "SIGNAL"
> that you NEED A LITTLE REST.

Helen's sincere interest in older people led many of them to see her as a faithful companion in time of crisis. This was certainly true for Rose, an elderly woman whose dream of Helen during an illness helped turn her experience of infirmity into a time of profound spiritual growth.

The Story of Rose

Rose wrote to Helen often. Although she never met her, Rose considered Helen her "dearest and best friend next to God." A single lady in her seventies, Rose had suffered a great deal, especially later in life. Around the time she began her correspondence with Helen, Rose developed a severe kidney problem and was hospitalized for a series of painful diagnostic tests. A few weeks after she returned home, she had to be rushed to the hospital again because of hemorrhaging. Heavily sedated to alleviate agonizing pain, Rose remembered little of the early days of her hospitalization. One thing she did remember, however, was a dream about Helen Steiner Rice. In her dream Helen came to her and kissed her, whispering, "I'm with you in spirit." Rose spent a long time in the hospital and all the while she was visited only twice by a neighbor, but during her convalescence she felt secure in the presence and support of God and of Helen Steiner Rice. She was especially encouraged when she received cards and poems from Helen in the mail and was truly moved by a letter in which Helen affirmed the deeply spiritual nature of Rose's experience.

> During these long weeks of suffering, you have known what it is to feel as if life were ebbing away . . . but when you took GOD'S HAND, all YOUR WEAKNESS left you and you felt STRONGER than you ever dreamed you would be! . . .
>
> Your suffering has not been wasted, for you accepted it as a precious GIFT. And you and I know that God is always our TRAVELING COMPANION in sorrow and in suffering and through it our KINSHIP with HIM is revealed.

In response Rose assured Helen that even before the card had reached her in the hospital, she had done what the poet advised her to do: "Let go and let God lead!"

> All in all my sojourn in the hospital was the most glorious and rewarding experience I have ever known. GOD IS SO REAL! JESUS IS

186

SO NEAR! ALL THE TIME! AND YOUR NAME—HELEN STEINER RICE—is in my prayers many times each day! . . . Our FATHER . . . knows what *you* and your writings mean to *me!*

For years Helen wrote poems for the retirement of her coworkers and friends without ever thinking of retirement as something she would eventually face herself. Yet she was sharp-witted enough to perceive the significance of this major transition in a person's life and she acknowledged it in one of the retirement verses she frequently used to wish her colleagues well:

> And while it "hurts the heart" to part
> From OLD ASSOCIATIONS
> And we miss our daily habits
> And familiar occupations,
> It's just life working out for us
> IN JUST THE WAY IT SHOULD—
> For there is NOTHING THAT GOD SENDS
> That is NOT MEANT FOR GOOD!

Eventually Helen had to recognize the fact that aging was taking a toll on her own body and her ability to work. She surrendered her position as editor at Gibson Greetings but took care to retain her old office at the company headquarters and went in every day to answer her mail. She also kept up her remarkable production of poetry, continuing to meet publishers' deadlines for new books of her verses. Chronic back and spinal problems, however, combined to slow her down. She came to believe that God was asking her to reflect on the pace of her life. In 1972 Helen had the chance to put her feelings into words when a Catholic nun wrote to her about a health problem. Helen answered:

My dear, you were just going TOO FAST, for, like myself, you are far too eager and zealous to help GOD. So you RAN instead of WALKED. You kept rushing and expending yourself in body and mind and used all your energy, and GOD just looked down and said, "I HAVE TO SLOW THIS GIRL DOWN."

I feel GOD has done the same to me, for the only way HE can slow you and I down is to take VERY FIRM and STERN STEPS.

While Helen saw a divine message in her enforced slower pace, she also credited spiritual resources for the energy that enabled her to keep writing despite her physical shortcomings. To her friend Mary Jane she confided,

I have become so terribly tired, and it is an effort for me to do things that used to afford me so much pleasure. Yet somehow I keep doing things that are beyond all my limitations. But through it all, I keep realizing that I could never have done the things I have done on my own strength and power, and I know my SPIRITUAL RESOURCES have been given to me by GOD and people all over the world who pray for me.

Even as Helen acknowledged her physical limitations, her illusion of security began crumbling around her. At the age of seventy-four Helen had to move. To her friend Audrey, Helen referred to the announcement of the Gibson Hotel's sudden closing as a "bombshell" that shattered her completely. She was at a loss as to what to do.

I am floundering around with no address and no definite plans. . . . But I do know for sure that GOD will manage it in HIS WAY. And since we both know that HIS WAY is always the right way, I will accept it as another GIFT OF HIS LOVE.

Helen survived the move from the Gibson thanks to the intervention of a good friend who found similar accommodations for her in the nearby Cincinnati Club, but she lost thirty pounds in the process. Later she was able to joke to a friend that there was a resemblance between her decline and the demolition of the hotel: "It's almost laughable to see them tearing the OLD GIBSON HOTEL down and to know that I am going right along with it!"

Growing Older Is Part of God's Plan

You can't hold back the dawn
Or stop the tides from flowing
Or keep a rose from withering
Or still a wind that's blowing
And time cannot be halted
In its swift and endless flight
For age is sure to follow youth
Like day comes after night.
And He who sets our span of years
And watches from above
Replaces youth and beauty
With peace and truth and love.
And then our souls are privileged
To see a hidden treasure
That in our youth escaped our eyes
In our pursuit of pleasure
So birthdays are but blessings
That open up the way
To the everlasting beauty
Of God's eternal day.

As she became increasingly infirm, Helen had to let go of her independence in much the same way she had to give up her position and her home. In 1977, after an extended hospitalization, Helen wrote to her friend Georgia about the stress brought on by this adjustment.

> My lifestyle has so completely changed that I find I am almost entirely dependent on the goodness, graciousness, and loving-kindness of my associates and friends, which, in itself, is something I must learn to accept as a fact and not feel awkward for being so helpless. . . . It takes a long time for a busy, active person to adjust when suddenly you have so many roadblocks thrown onto THE HIGHWAY OF LIFE that traveling on your own becomes impossible.

One of Helen's greatest joys had always been the letters she received from people all around the world who found comfort in her poems. Hard as it sometimes was, she responded to those letters and kept up a steady stream of encouragement to those in need. By the spring of 1977, however, she discovered that she would have to begin letting go of her letter writing. She wrote her friend Audrey, "One of the things that troubles me the most is that with all my limitations, it seems I am so handicapped in answering all the lovely letters that come in to me in such great abundance every day."

In every letting-go experience, Helen placed herself in God's hands. And no matter what the situation or her personal limitations, she expressed gratitude—to God, to her friends, to those who loved her work. She thanked God for giving her the words that enabled her to write poems, for the sunshine and rain, and for problems that compelled her to grow spiritually. At the same time she thanked her friends for their many kindnesses, great and small. "Just to be remembered fills me with GLORIOUS GRATITUDE," she wrote enthusiastically to one confidant. She also sincerely expressed her gratitude to the fans who remembered her during the Christmas holidays, even when she became so frail that it took her four months to finish writing her thank-you notes.

Above all else, Helen was determined to conform her will to God's and to accept every setback as an opportunity to grow in faith. "My physical limitations seem to multiply," she wrote to friends in September 1977, "but I feel in my heart that GOD has enriched me SPIRITUALLY, for I think GOD often takes away our comforts and privileges to make us better Christians." The experience of letting go that Helen faced so often as she aged has been a difficult one for Vincent, who lost the comforts that once sustained him. At first it proved almost impossible for him to accept how aging drastically altered his life, but he slowly adjusted. Now he finds that Helen's poems really make a difference when it comes to filling the emptiness that often plagues him.

The Story of Vincent

Vincent has learned the basic lessons of letting go in the aftermath of a stroke. During the period of his recovery Vincent had to move out of his home and because he would be gone for a long time, all his possessions, including his Helen Steiner Rice books, were placed in storage, given away, or lost. "About all I can do for myself nowadays is read, write, dress myself, and feed myself," Vincent writes. He found himself longing every day for inspirational thoughts, poems, and prayers. Luckily for him, he received the book *Lovingly* as a gift. He read it avidly, and at the end he found verses that reassured him and promised to brighten his days in the future.

> God's grace is all-sufficient
> For both the young and old,
> For the lonely and the timid
> For the brash and for the bold—
> His love knows no exceptions,
> So never feel excluded

191

No matter who or what you are
Your name has been included.

The Story of Edward

Prayer also matters more than anything else to Edward. Like Vincent, he recently suffered a stroke, and his problems were magnified by the serious illness of his wife. But despite all his cares and worries, the poem "Prayers Can't Be Answered Unless They Are Prayed" has inspired him to take heart.

So whatever is wrong with your life today,
You'll find a solution if you kneel down and pray . . .
. . . pray for a purpose to make life worth living
And pray for the joy of unselfish giving.
For great is your gladness and rich your reward
When you make your life's purpose the choice of the Lord.

For Bessie, Helen's message of cheerfulness makes the path of infirmity a smoother one, while for Agnes, it is the emphasis on gratitude that she finds so inspiring.

The Story of Bessie

Bessie lives in a nursing home. For years Helen Steiner Rice's poems have helped her maintain an attitude of acceptance and appreciation. Recently she asked the Homebound Librarian to collect the latest books of Helen's poems and bring them to the nursing home, for Bessie is convinced that even though Helen's message has a universal appeal, it is especially important for those struggling with infirmity. She describes Helen as "the dear little lady who always knew the right thing to say to comfort, cheer, and lift hearts who so badly need a lift along life's way especially when they are no longer able to go the places they would." Bessie also thanks God for the people around her, "for

Prayers Can't Be Answered Unless They Are Prayed

Life without purpose is barren indeed—
There can't be a harvest unless you plant seed,
There can't be attainment unless there's a goal,
And man's but a robot unless there's a soul . . .
If we send no ships out, no ships will come in,
And unless there's a contest, nobody can win . . .
For games can't be won unless they are played,
And prayers can't be answered unless they are prayed . . .
So whatever is wrong with your life today,
You'll find a solution if you kneel down and pray
Not just for pleasure, enjoyment and health,
Not just for honors and prestige and wealth . . .
But pray for a purpose to make life worth living
And pray for the joy of unselfish giving.
For great is your gladness and rich your reward
When you make your life's purpose the choice of the Lord.

all his loving, caring people who don't wait too late to say the things they should to those who mean the most."

The Story of Agnes

The words of the poem "Good Morning, God" have special meaning to Agnes, who like Bessie resides in a nursing home. Agnes suffered a bad fall and was seriously injured. That is the reason these lines of the poem are so meaningful to her:

> Father, I am well aware
> I can't make it on my own
> So take my hand and hold it tight
> For I can't walk alone!

Her fall broke her glasses, bruised her face and eye, and hurt her right side "from ankle to hip" but it certainly did not break her spirit. She remains cheerful and optimistic, is grateful for the workers and nurses who care for her, and gives sincere thanks to God that she was not more seriously injured. "Lucky I didn't break my hip," she writes. "I would be laid up a long time. I say my prayers. God was with me."

By September 1979 Helen Steiner Rice had reached the point in her life where she joked with a friend that the list of her ailments had grown too long to fit on the insurance form. She had just broken another vertebra in her back when struggling to lift herself out of bed, she explained, but she recounted this latest setback with the same spirit of gratitude to God that always accompanied any discussion of her health: "I guess you get used to anything and I think God IS WONDERFUL to give me the stamina to just KEEP ON KEEPING ON."

Even at age seventy-nine Helen still tried to get to her office at Gibson Greetings as often as possible to answer letters from friends and her devoted fans. Finally, in April 1980 Helen suffered

Dark Shadows Fall in the Lives of Us All

Sickness and sorrow come to us all,
But through it we grow and learn to "stand tall"
For trouble is "part and parcel of life"
And no man can grow without struggle and strife,
And the more we endure with patience and grace
The stronger we grow and the more we can face
And the more we can face the greater our love,
And with love in our hearts we are more conscious of
The pain and the sorrow in lives everywhere
So it is through trouble that we learn how to share.

a terrible misfortune: She broke her hip. She was sent to Franciscan Terrace, a highly respected nursing and residence facility in suburban Cincinnati, to convalesce. Helen spent her final months there. One of her visitors during that time was a woman who had known Helen for decades and whom Helen fondly called "Goldilocks." Goldilocks was not at all surprised to see in Helen the same bright and positive spirit that had been the hallmark of her entire life.

The Story of Goldilocks

"Goldilocks," whose real name is Marjorie Stricker Nelson, first met Helen Steiner Rice in 1948. Marjorie was a teenager then, working at the Kroger's Grocery on Fountain Square in downtown Cincinnati. Helen evidently had a special fondness for Fritos corn chips, and she customarily stopped at Kroger's to buy them on her way home to her room at the Gibson Hotel after leaving the office. When Helen walked into the store, Marjorie remembers, "everyone would stop what they were doing" and "everything got quiet. She just looked beautiful," and everybody fell in love with her. As she did with many of her friends, Helen gave Marjorie a nickname. Helen called her "Goldilocks" because of her curly blond hair.

When Marjorie was married, Helen sent her a beautiful wedding card, but when Marjorie and her husband began to raise their family, she lost touch with Helen for a few years. Still, Marjorie never forgot Helen or her many kindnesses and in 1953 she wrote to Helen just to make her aware of what knowing her had meant. The letter arrived at just the right moment for Helen, who explained why when she wrote back, "Dear Goldilocks":

It was near the end of the day, and I was a little wearily sad recognizing, as I so often do, how difficult it is to spread sunshine in a

196

Golden Years of Life

God in His loving and all-wise way
Makes the heart that once was young and gay
Serene and more gentle and less restless, too,
Content to remember the joys it once knew . . .
And all that we sought on "the pathway of pleasure"
Becomes but a memory to cherish and treasure—
The fast pace grows slower and the spirit serene,
And our souls can envision what our eyes have not
    seen . . .
And so while "life's springtime" is sweet to recall,
The "autumn of life" is the best time of all,
For our wild youthful yearnings all gradually cease
And God fills our days with beauty and peace!

world that is so callous and cold. But when I started to read your letter, things suddenly seemed to be much more worthwhile, and it made me very keenly aware that God is love and He is everywhere.

Helen ended her letter with a little verse that reminded the young mother of her own goodness:

> Here's something I must tell you
> For it's very, very true . . .
> The "lovely things" you saw in me . . .
> Were just a *REFLECTION OF YOU.*

Marjorie has saved that letter for more than forty years and she never lost touch with Helen Steiner Rice again. During Helen's final year of life Marjorie often went to visit her at Franciscan Terrace. Marjorie borrowed a hymnbook from her church and took it to the nursing home. There, she and Helen would sit and sing hymns together. Frequently the nurses' aides would come in and join them.

One day when Marjorie visited, she brought with her a request from a woman whose aged, ailing mother was a faithful Helen Steiner Rice fan of many years. Would Helen autograph a piece of paper for the elderly woman, Marjorie asked? Helen instructed Marjorie to open the closet in her room and select a book of poems for the lady. Helen then signed the book and sent it back with Marjorie as a special gift.

This sort of thoughtfulness and generosity did not surprise Marjorie. Helen's action was consistent with the behavior she had witnessed for decades. To Marjorie, Helen Steiner Rice was simply a rare and wonderful person, and what made her so above all else was that she stayed the same through all the years. Neither her fame nor her pain had changed her. Helen remained caring, sensitive, humble, and compassionate. "She was a beautiful person," Marjorie remembers. "She was like sunshine until she died."

How does someone remain "like sunshine" in the face of aging and infirmity? It certainly is no easy task, but Helen's lifetime example, just like her verses, shows the way. She summarized it nicely in her poem "Give Me the Contentment of Acceptance" when she wrote that all God ever required of her

> Was not a "servant" the world admired
> But a humbled heart and a sanctified soul
> Whose only mission and purpose and goal
> Was to be content with whatever God sends.

Acceptance, then, is the key to healing the pain of aging and infirmity. This of course does not mean resignation or helpless surrender, nor does it mean that we should court suffering by foregoing appropriate medical support. What it does mean is that when we have done our part, given our very best, then we should relinquish the outcome into God's hands in good cheer, in gratitude, and in peace. We remain like sunshine, then, by radiating love and warmth to the world around us, whether life delivers what is to our liking or not.

Helen's Pattern for Healing the Pain of Infirmity

1. Recognizing limitations.

Ask yourself: Do I understand that God often asks me to let go of the expectations I have of myself? Can I accept that in letting go I am showing faith in God's plan?

2. Maintaining a cheerful outlook.

Ask yourself: Can I laugh at myself? Can I be cheerful even when I am discouraged? Can I express gratitude for my life and those who have touched it?

3. Growing in acceptance.

Ask yourself: Am I able to accept whatever God sends? Can I surrender to a higher plan even when I do not understand it? Can I grow in contentment by seeking God's will in the face of every obstacle?

Eight

Your Healing Touch

So if you found some beauty
In any word or line
It's just your soul's reflection
In proximity to mine.

Over the years many people told Helen Steiner Rice that her poetry healed them from life's wounds. All of them fervently believed that it was true. But whenever she heard such high praise, Helen knew in her heart that something else had transpired. She knew that what people saw in her and in her verses was merely a reflection of the Divine Healer. Helen thought of herself as a channel through which God administered a healing touch.

The Healing Touch is about Helen's ability to touch our spiritual eyes, as Christ touched the eyes of the blind men in the Gospel of Matthew. It is about her ability to awaken and encourage soul-sight in all of us when our vision is focused on the pain of personal events. Only through soul-sight do we see God at

With His Love

If you found any beauty
In the poems in this book
Or some peace and comfort
In a word or line,
Don't give me the praise
Or worldly acclaim
For the words that you read
Are not mine . . .
I borrowed them all
To share with you
From our Heavenly Father above,
And the joy that you felt
Was God speaking to you
As He flooded your heart
With His Love.

work in our heartaches. Only through soul-sight can we develop a healing touch ourselves.

To become a healer is painful, challenging, and costly. To become a healer we must not only suffer but also allow our suffering to change us. We must view everyday life symbolically, look for the face of God in every person, and recognize the hand of God in every event. We must live our Christian faith literally and thus believe in God and God's goodness under all circumstances, even those that distress us the most. We must love one another as Christ loved—without condition or exception—even when the "other" seems most unlovable. This is not a program for the faint of heart. Yet this is exactly how we heal our wounds, the wounds that occur when our hopes, dreams, and expectations of how life would be or should be collide with the way life actually is. This is how we, like Helen, acquire a healing touch.

One person who tries daily to see God at work in his life is Bobby Smith, a Navajo Indian. Bobby finds in the words of Helen Steiner Rice help and inspiration to persevere in this mission. Our final chapter opens with his story.

The Story of Bobby

Mesas, canyons, buttes, and deserts form the landscape of the Navajo Reservation in the southwestern United States, where Bobby Smith was born in Cousins, New Mexico, in 1938. It is not surprising that Bobby finds comfort, healing, and peace in the writing of Helen Steiner Rice, for deep religious feeling and the love of beauty in all its forms permeate the Navajo culture.

Bobby first saw Helen's poems on greeting cards twenty years ago in a small shop in Gallup, New Mexico, not far from his home. Her verses touched his heart, and he believes God uses Helen to touch other hearts as well. Helen's poems encouraged Bobby in his decision to become a Christian in 1980 and they continue to affirm his faith, a faith to which he testifies joyfully, "I believe in my loving Lord Jesus Christ."

Helen's poems bring a sense of spiritual calm to Bobby and form a solid bridge between his bedrock native traditions and his love of Christ. The Navajo way emphasizes harmony and balance, peace and beauty, as this sacred song illustrates:

> Now I walk with Talking God
> With goodness and beauty in all things around me I go;
> With goodness and beauty I follow immortality,
> Thus being I, I go.

That song carries a message closely akin to one of the Helen Steiner Rice verses that Bobby cherishes.

> May the Love of God surround you
> May His peace be all around you
> And may your day be blest
> With everything that's happiest.

Bobby writes that he has faith in "God's Great Love" and finds joy in his work repairing shoes and boots for the people of Gallup. "It is wonderful how our Lord Jesus Christ is," he says. "He walks with me and talks with me every day of life."

In the Navajo tradition healers help the sick and ailing return to harmony within themselves and with the world around them. This is what Helen Steiner Rice does so very well in the Christian tradition. Bobby's favorite among all of Helen's poems is one of the shortest, but it conveys a powerful message emphasizing the need for harmony:

> Peace on earth will come to stay
> When we live Christmas every day.

It is a firm faith in God that sustains us when we must witness and experience life's pain. Faith, according to Helen, helps us learn

The Master Builder

God is the Master Builder
Whose Plan is perfect and true,
And when God sends you sorrow
It's part of the plan for you
For all things work together
To achieve the Master Plan
And God in heaven knows what's best
For woman and for man.

A Prayer for Humility

Take me and break me and make me, dear God,
Just what you want me to be—
Give me the strength to accept what You send
And eyes with the vision to see
All the small arrogant ways that I have
And the vain little things that I do,
Make me aware that I'm often concerned
More with myself than with You,
Uncover before me my weakness and greed
And help me to search deep inside
So I may discover how easy it is
To be selfishly lost in my pride—
And then in Thy goodness and mercy
Look down on this weak, erring one
And tell me that I am forgiven
For all I've so willfully done,
And teach me to humbly start following
The path that the dear Savior trod
So I'll find at the end of life's journey
"A home in the city of God."

from our suffering; it also invites us to wait patiently in the expectation that our lives are unfolding in new ways in accordance with God's plan. This is at the heart of one of Helen's most popular poems, "The Master Builder," which asks the reader to believe, "When God sends you sorrow, it's part of the plan for you."

Helen realized that so much of life's pain is caused by our limited ways of thinking, our unwillingness to open ourselves to another perspective or let go of what we want and what we plan. She realized that the only way to let the divine will control her life was for her human will to be broken, so she asked God to break her so that she could develop soul-sight:

> Take me and break me and make me, dear God,
> Just what you want me to be—
> Give me the strength to accept what You send
> And eyes with the vision to see.

She understood that her own pain was truly the way to God; moreover it was the way to becoming a healer. Accepting her pain in faith enabled Helen to see beyond the limitations of human awareness and develop a divine perspective. She understood that with a shift in attitude, a change in perception, and a willingness to drop our personal controls and trust God's wisdom, life's most painful experiences could become the transforming events that allowed God's grace to flow through us to others. Faith, she counseled, supports us as we transform our pain. Then as a result of our suffering we can be blessed with the ability to ease the pain of others who also face the confusion and disorientation that occurs when divine reality steps in front of our human fantasies.

Helen's poems teach us how to live by faith: Every event that occurs, every person we encounter, every disappointment or joy we experience is an invitation from God to grow spiritually. Living in faith requires minute-by-minute surrender; it means seeing everything as a gift of God's love, no matter how much it breaks our human heart. Only with this kind of faith can we empty ourselves of human expectation, and the more we rid ourselves of our own desires, the more brightly the healing light of God shines through us. Helen Steiner Rice subscribed whole-heartedly to Saint Paul's belief "that in all things God works for the good of those who love him" (Rom. 8:28).

For Helen the natural outgrowth of healing her own pain was an outpouring of compassion for the pain of others. That compassion manifested itself most clearly as the unselfish love Helen offered to those who knew her personally and to the hundreds of people with whom she corresponded. She practiced love in its highest form: without conditions and without a private agenda. Her books bore her daily prayer:

> Show me the way not to fortune or fame
> Not how to win laurels or praise for my name
> But show me the way to spread "The Great Story"
> That Thine is the kingdom and power and glory.

To live a life of love at this level requires conscious decision-making in the myriad events that occur each day. One person who watched Helen Steiner Rice do this was her minister and close friend, Rev. Ernie Bein.

The Story of Ernie

In the 1970s young Ernie Bein served as the pastor of Wesley Chapel, the Methodist church Helen Steiner Rice regularly attended in downtown Cincinnati. The lessons he learned from Helen during the hours they spent in conversation remain with him to this day. "The thing that made Helen Steiner Rice special was the Spirit of God—the Spirit of Christ—within her," he recollects. Reverend Bein had many occasions to see

207

the Spirit at work and in fact became the channel through which Helen touched many lives with healing and with love.

Helen was especially devoted to the congregation at Wesley. She asked Ernie to make her aware of any special needs he saw arise within that assembly if he thought she could help the parishioners. He deeply appreciated her offer and took her up on it. As a result Helen quietly and unobtrusively shared her financial resources over the years, and Ernie judiciously distributed the money she sent to him. For example, he provided food for a desperately poor family of seven and for an elderly woman, he assisted an indigent mother with a ten-month-old son, he financed baseball uniforms for young men who could not afford them, he sent allowances to prisoners, and he paid the tuition for a promising university student. There were other charitable acts too numerous to mention. Helen was such a loyal and generous benefactor that she once fretted in a letter to Ernie that she feared he was disappointed that she had not given to the church's Fine Arts Fund. "I am not at all disappointed," he hastened to assure her. "You have your priorities straight—our first call is still to express God's love in any way we can to the lives of other people." This surely was the first call of Helen Steiner Rice.

Rev. Ernie Bein saw God's love express itself through Helen Steiner Rice in many and varied ways. Her generosity to his church was only one of them. Her sensitivity to the pain of others was another. He found her crying at her desk at Gibson Greetings one day, distressed at the heartache of a young widow whose husband had died unexpectedly. No doubt she could especially identify with this woman's grief because of her own experience, but it was Helen's nature to empathize with the suffering of others. Committed though she was to easing the pain she witnessed as well as she could, Helen often felt inadequate for the task. "It really just tears my heart out not to be able to respond to the instant crises of those who are in deep need," she wrote to Ernie Bein in February 1977. He was amazed at her capacity for caring, to say nothing of her stamina and energy despite her own health problems. Responding to her letter as soon as he recovered from an illness of his own, Ernie wrote, "When my energy fails I think of the stamina you have in the face of your pain and I find my little ills infinitesimal."

Truly it seemed that Helen Steiner Rice was propelled by a spiritual energy that grew and aided her even as her body failed. And yet Helen's assessment of herself always seemed to leave her far short of her goal. "It seems that I DO SO LITTLE when I want to do so much," she wrote to Ernie. Physically weak as Helen was, she did recognize in herself a great strength, the outpouring of her own love and its divine connection. She assured Ernie in August 1977, "My greatest peace of soul comes from trying to reach out in love by sharing whatever I have with other people. Somehow it seems to open the way for A CLOSER WALK WITH GOD."

Helen's daily life reflected nothing but love to Ernie Bein. "The Christ in her was always present," is the beautiful way he expresses it. He was amazed during the final years of her life, when Helen was in constant pain, how she continued her correspondence commitments and managed to write new poems without complaint or remorse. She once explained to him that "JOY can be found in the darkest hours of our deepest sorrow, for everything is a cause for JOY when THE LORD has hold of our hand."

One of Helen's greatest joys was assisting young people from her church who were preparing for the ministry. In July 1975 Rev. Bein wrote Helen a letter intended to bring someone special to her attention:

Do you remember Gloria Burke? . . . She has worked with the children and youth of our church for several years. . . . Gloria has been trying to deal with what seems to be an authentic call to the ministry. She has decided to pursue that call. . . . I am sure you will share with us the joy of this decision by one of our young people.

Since the young woman's resources were limited, Ernie hoped that Helen might be willing to relieve the financial burden of seminary training for her. He was not disappointed, for Helen did indeed remember Gloria Burke well. She responded enthusiastically to Ernie's request:

> If I can help this dedicated young lady to give herself entirely to God and not to use her talents searching for PERSONAL PLEASURE, PRESTIGE, AND POWER, I shall feel I have at least tried in a small way to help her and encourage her to keep on being the lovely young lady she is.

Helen's belief in Gloria as a young woman of great promise was amply rewarded. Helen wrote to Ernie Bein in March 1976:

> I am so glad you told me that Gloria Burke needed a little assistance. I have never made a better investment, for faithfully that girl has written to me and told me how she's getting along at college. *I* am just *honored* and *happy* to have had a *little part* in making it possible for her to be studying for the ministry.

Gloria Burke became Rev. Gloria Brooks. Her story about the impact of Helen Steiner Rice on her life was recounted in the first chapter of this book. Ernie Bein, Helen's friend and minister, was the person who steadfastly encouraged Gloria to follow her heart and pursue her religious vocation. Helen Steiner Rice's human chain of love and kindness has circled the lives of both Gloria and Ernie and left a permanent healing touch.

Ernie Bein believes Helen's poem "The Soul of Man" sums up her perspective on God and humankind. It emphasizes her belief that love must be a part of all our encounters with one another if we are to live as a healed, whole people:

> And in the Father's Holy Sight
> No man is yellow, black, or white,
> And peace on earth cannot be found
> Until we meet on common ground
> And every man becomes a brother
> Who worships God and loves all others.

But Rev. Ernie Bein does not recite Helen's poems when he speaks of her these days to his congregation in northern Ohio. It is the memory of the deep understanding between Helen and him that he prefers to share:

I share with my congregations those special, shared, personal times, thoughts and experiences that are so precious. Everyone can read her poetry. But she was my friend. So I share about my friend, whose personhood and life were and are ten times more inspiring to me than anything she ever wrote.

Helen Steiner Rice continues to inspire—and to touch with healing power—the lives of people all over the world, people like Ernie Bein and Gloria Brooks and all the others whose stories appear in these pages, and countless more as well.

The Soul of Man

Every man has a deep heart need
That cannot be filled with doctrine or creed,
For the soul of man knows nothing more
Than just that he is longing for
A haven that is safe and sure,
A fortress where he feels secure,
An island in this sea of strife
Away from all the storms of life . . .
Oh, God of love, who sees us all
You are so great! We are so small!
Hear man's universal prayer
Crying to You in despair—
"Save my soul and grant me peace,
Let my restless murmurings cease,
God of love—Forgive! Forgive!
Teach me how to truly live,
Ask me not my race or creed,
Just take me in my hour of need,
And let me know You love me, too,
And that I am a part of You" . . .
And someday may man realize
That all the earth, the seas, and skies
Belong to God who made us all,
The rich, the poor, the great, the small,
And in the Father's Holy Sight
No man is yellow, black, or white,
And peace on earth cannot be found
Until we meet on common ground
And every man becomes a brother
Who worships God and loves all others.

Helen's Pattern for Becoming a Healer

1. Seeing life symbolically.

Ask yourself: Do I understand my life symbolically? Can I identify the seasons of my soul and the resurrection cycle of birth, death, and renewal in the events of my life? Can I see the face of God in every person and the hand of God in every occurrence?

2. Accepting in faith that God has a divine plan.

Ask yourself: Can I accept that God's wisdom is guiding the unfolding of my life? Can I let go of my need for a logical, human explanation for the events of life and instead accept in faith that God guides even those things I cannot understand?

3. Choosing to live life with love.

Ask yourself: Do I believe in the transforming power of love? Am I willing to love others as Christ loved? Do I understand that the extent to which I reflect God's love is the result of my daily choices?

Afterword

This book opened with the twelve healing attitudes of Helen Steiner Rice. These are the themes she turned to over and over in her poetry. They are perceptions she used to guide her own life. Verse came naturally to Helen, so much so that she often spoke and wrote in rhyme even when she was not thinking about composing poems. It seems appropriate at this point to return to those healing attitudes and to couple each of them with a brief verse by Helen.

1. God loves you. You are never outside God's care.

> God's love knows no exceptions
> So never feel excluded
> No matter who or what you are
> Your name has been included.

2. God hears your every prayer. You are never alone if you can talk to God.

> God's presence is ever beside you
> As near as the reach of your hand
> You have but to tell God your troubles
> There is nothing God won't understand.

3. God works through you. Loving yourself
and others is God at work.

> It's a wonderful world and it always will be
> If we keep our eyes open and focused to see
> The wonderful things we are capable of
> When we open our hearts to God and God's love.

4. God's plan is unfolding even when you do not
understand it. Surrender your will to God.

> Wise people accept whatever God sends
> Willing to yield like a storm-tossed tree bends
> Knowing that God never makes a mistake
> So whatever God sends they are willing to take.

5. God's grace is always found in the present
moment. Stay focused on the present.

> All I need live for
> Is this one little minute
> For life's here and now
> And eternity's in it.

6. God has not asked only you to cope with
problems. They are part of every person's life.
Refuse to indulge in self-pity.

> All that is required of us
> Whenever things go wrong
> Is to trust in God implicitly
> With a faith that's deep and strong.

7. Rid yourself of negative thinking. You cannot enjoy life when you are filled with complaints.

> Supposin' the worst things will happen
> Only helps to make them come true
> And you darken the bright, happy moments
> That the dear Lord has given to you.

8. Be grateful for your many blessings.

> Help us to remember that
> The key to Life and Living
> Is to make each prayer a prayer of thanks
> And every day Thanksgiving.

9. Be kind. Acts of kindness transform the world.

> Kindness is a virtue
> Given by the Lord,
> It pays dividends in happiness
> And joy is its reward.

10. Support one another. All of us are a valued part of God's creation.

> When we "give ourselves away"
> In sacrifice and love,
> We are "laying up rich treasures"
> In God's kingdom up above.

11. Be cheerful. Happiness is a choice you make every day.

> When the heart is cheerful
> It cannot be filled with fear

And without fear the way ahead
Seems more distinct and clear.

12. Learn from adversity. Your troubles are great teachers.

The things that cause the heart to ache
Until we feel that it must break
Become the strength by which we climb
To higher heights that are sublime.

Helen Steiner Rice realized that we enter the realm of the divine through our suffering. In this realm sorrow both hurts and heals us; it breaks us but also builds our strength. Helen explained it in her usual uncomplicated way—God gives us the healing touch in exchange for our pain.

Blessings come in many guises
That God alone in love devises
And sorrow, which we dread so much
Can bring a very healing touch.

Helen Steiner Rice administered her healing touch by practicing her Christian beliefs in every circumstance of her daily living. King Solomon once reflected on the personification of wisdom in words that perfectly describe Helen's life: "She instructed us in the understanding of God."

There Are Blessings in Everything

God speaks to us in many ways,
Altering our lives, our plans and days,
And His blessings come in many guises
That He alone in love devises,
And sorrow, which we dread so much,
Can bring a very healing touch . . .
For when we fail to heed His voice
We leave the Lord no other choice
Except to use a firm, stern hand
To make us know He's in command . . .
For on the wings of loss and pain,
The peace we often sought in vain
Will come to us with sweet surprise,
For God is merciful and wise . . .
And through dark hours of tribulation
God gives us time for meditation,
And nothing can be counted loss
Which teaches us to bear our cross.

Ronald Pollitt is a retired professor of history and college dean. He is the author of several books and articles.

Virginia Wiltse is an award-winning former television journalist who is now a freelance writer.